# Backyard Abundance for Greenhouse Beginners

A Guide to Avoid Common Greenhouse Gardening Pitfalls: Create a Healthy, Self-Sufficient Hobby and Dynamic Business While Enjoying Your Personal Sanctuary

**Jessie Kelias**

© Copyright 2022 - All rights reserved.

The content contained within this book may not be reproduced, duplicated or transmitted without direct written permission from the author or the publisher.

Under no circumstances will any blame or legal responsibility be held against the publisher, or author, for any damages, reparation, or monetary loss due to the information contained within this book, either directly or indirectly.

Legal Notice:

This book is copyright protected. It is only for personal use. You cannot amend, distribute, sell, use, quote or paraphrase any part, or the content within this book, without the consent of the author or publisher.

Disclaimer Notice:

Please note the information contained within this document is for educational and entertainment purposes only. All effort has been executed to present accurate, up to date, reliable, complete information. No warranties of any kind are declared or implied. Readers acknowledge that the author is not engaged in the rendering of legal, financial, medical or professional advice. The content within this book has been derived from various sources. Please consult a licensed professional before attempting any techniques outlined in this book.

By reading this document, the reader agrees that under no circumstances is the author responsible for any losses, direct or indirect, that are incurred as a result of the use of the information contained within this document, including, but not limited to, errors, omissions, or inaccuracies.

# Table of Contents

**INTRODUCTION** .................................................................................. 1
    WHAT IS A BACKYARD GREENHOUSE? .......................................... 3
    GREENHOUSES BOOST YOUR HEALTH ........................................... 4
        *Stress Relief* ........................................................................... 4
        *Fitness and Exercise* ............................................................. 5
        *Sunlight and Vitamin D* ........................................................ 5
        *Mental Health* ...................................................................... 6
        *Community* ........................................................................... 6
    THE ALLURE OF THE HARVEST ..................................................... 7

**CHAPTER 1: PREPARING YOURSELF** ............................................. 9
    CHOOSING THE RIGHT LOCATION ............................................... 10
    TOOLS OF THE TRADE ............................................................... 12
        *Garden Spade* ..................................................................... 13
        *Garden Trowel* ................................................................... 14
        *Garden Shears* .................................................................... 14
        *Gardening Gloves* ............................................................... 15
        *Optional Tools* .................................................................... 16
    WHAT TO EXPECT ..................................................................... 17

**CHAPTER 2: DESIGNING THE GREENHOUSE** ............................. 19
    TYPES OF GREENHOUSES .......................................................... 20
        *Cold Frame* ......................................................................... 20
        *Attached* ............................................................................. 22
        *Freestanding* ...................................................................... 24
    BUILDING A GREENHOUSE ........................................................ 26
        *Flooring* .............................................................................. 26
        *Windows* ............................................................................ 27
        *Location* ............................................................................. 29
    BUYING A GREENHOUSE ........................................................... 30
    ACCESSORIES TO CONSIDER ...................................................... 32
        *Thermometers* ................................................................... 32
        *Ventilation* ......................................................................... 34
        *Shelving and Storage* ......................................................... 35

THE RIGHT GREENHOUSE FOR YOU ............................................................ 36

# CHAPTER 3: PICKING YOUR PRODUCE ...............................................39

SOME FRUITY OPTIONS ........................................................................... 40
    *Strawberries* ............................................................................... 40
    *Bananas* ...................................................................................... 41
    *Peaches* ....................................................................................... 43
    *Oranges* ...................................................................................... 44
GROWING YOUR VEGGIES ....................................................................... 44
    *Corn* ............................................................................................. 45
    *Cucumbers* ................................................................................. 46
    *Root Vegetables (carrots, potatoes, etc.)* ............................... 47
    *Leafy Vegetables (Kale, Lettuce, etc.)* ..................................... 49
HERBACEOUS TENANTS ........................................................................... 50
    *Rosemary* .................................................................................... 50
    *Thyme* .......................................................................................... 52
    *Basil* ............................................................................................. 53
    *Parsley* ........................................................................................ 54
STARTING FROM SEEDS ........................................................................... 55
MAXIMIZING GERMINATION ................................................................... 57

# CHAPTER 4: GREENHOUSE MAINTENANCE .......................................59

CREATING THE RIGHT ENVIRONMENT ..................................................... 60
    *Water* ........................................................................................... 60
    *Temperature & Humidity* .......................................................... 62
    *Light* ............................................................................................ 63
    *Soil* .............................................................................................. 64
CLEANING AND UPKEEP ........................................................................... 65
    *Common Repairs* ....................................................................... 67
    *Managing Mold* ......................................................................... 68
PLANNING YOUR SPACE ........................................................................... 70
YOUR DAILY CHECKLIST ........................................................................... 71
    *Daily Greenhouse Maintenance Checklist* ............................. 72

# CHAPTER 5: GOOD PEST - BAD PEST .................................................73

BAD PESTS ............................................................................................... 73
    *Aphids* ......................................................................................... 73
    *Thrips* .......................................................................................... 75
    *Slugs/snails* ................................................................................ 76
    *Whiteflies* ................................................................................... 77
GOOD PESTS ............................................................................................ 78

  *Bumblebee* ............................................................................. *78*
  *Praying Mantis* .................................................................... *79*
  *Lady Beetle (Ladybug)* ....................................................... *80*
  *Lacewing* .............................................................................. *81*

## CHAPTER 6: DEALING WITH DISEASE ................................... 83
 COMMON GREENHOUSE DISEASES ..................................................... 83
  *Bacterial Wilt* ....................................................................... *84*
  *Erwinia* ................................................................................. *85*
  *Root Rot* ............................................................................... *86*
  *Powdery Mildew* ................................................................. *87*
  *Impatiens Necrotic Spot Virus (INSV)* ............................... *88*
 AN OUNCE OF PREVENTION .............................................................. 89

## CHAPTER 7: HARVEST TIME! ................................................ 93
 TIMING IS EVERYTHING ..................................................................... 93
 SIZE YOUR CROP .............................................................................. 94
 STAY ATTENTIVE .............................................................................. 95
 SOME BASIC TECHNIQUES ................................................................. 95
  *Pinching vs. Pruning* .......................................................... *95*
  *Minimizing Damage* ........................................................... *96*
  *Washing Practices* .............................................................. *97*

## CHAPTER 8: STORAGE AND CARE ........................................ 99
 LONG TERM PRESERVATION ............................................................. 99
  *Dry Storage* ......................................................................... *99*
  *Canning* ............................................................................. *101*
  *Freezing* ............................................................................ *102*
  *Drying* ............................................................................... *104*
  *Fermenting* ....................................................................... *106*
 MONITORING YOUR HARVEST ........................................................ 107

## CHAPTER 9: PULLING A PROFIT ......................................... 109
 NETWORKING AND CONNECTION ................................................... 109
  *Meeting Potential Customers* .......................................... *109*
  *Get To Know The Demand* ............................................... *110*
  *Be Transparent* ................................................................. *111*
 DESIGNING YOUR BUSINESS ............................................................ 112
  *Modified CSA* .................................................................... *112*
  *Online Market* .................................................................. *113*
  *Farmer's Markets* ............................................................. *114*

*Personal* ................................................................................ *116*

## CHAPTER 10: MAKING IT LAST ........................................................ 121
FAIL TO PLAN, PLAN TO FAIL .................................................................. 121
YEAR-ROUND PRODUCTION ................................................................... 122
*Alternating Crops*............................................................................ *122*
*Stagger Planting*............................................................................. *123*
*Planting in Season* .......................................................................... *125*

## CONCLUSION ............................................................................... 127

## REFERENCES ................................................................................ 133
IMAGE REFERENCES ............................................................................ 136

# A Special Gift to My Readers

Included in the purchase of this book is

my free guide to keeping your greenhouse garden cool during the

hot summer months.

Click the link below to let me know which email you'd like your freebie delivered to.

Many thanks!

Jessie

https://jessiekelias1313.activehosted.com/f/1

# Introduction

I'm going to throw a disturbing number at you.

**Seventy.** 7-0.

That number represents the percentage of fresh produce sold in the US that contains the residue of potentially harmful pesticides even after washing (Holden, 2019).

Go ahead, look it up.

I'm not going to bore you with details about how these pesticides can affect our health. Instead, I want to share with you all the benefits I've discovered as I've explored a much better option: growing your own food.

Hear me out! Have you ever wanted to try something drastically different from anything you've ever known? I remember my life in New York City vividly. I can still smell the city and hear the loud rhythm of urban life. I was a city girl, and even though this place was home, I needed a change.

Perhaps you're a little like me. You're hoping for a change as well. You feel an inner push motivating you to step out into something different. Maybe you're trying to improve your health, you want to explore a new business venture, or you're looking for a fresh and challenging hobby. That's why you picked up this book. Like me, you're looking for the next step. Or, maybe, it's your first.

At twenty-five, I left my busy and familiar city life to find that next step. I moved to a new location in upstate New York, a small town where everyone knew each other, and I took that first step into something different.

I started a traditional garden. I'd explored this hobby before, because back then, NYC didn't offer all the same culinary delights that it now does for vegetarians like me. Besides that, I was concerned about pesticides and the quality of food I was buying and consuming. I have always dreamed of growing my own food. When I got started growing small, simple, and chemical-free produce, I was instantly in love.

I was happy to bring this hobby to a brand new home. Having a fair amount of success with my summer garden and feeling inspired to have healthy and organic produce year-round, I decided to try something new.

If there's one thing that gardening has taught me, it's that you will get out of it what you put in. I was determined to be as self-sufficient as possible. So, I decided to try greenhouse gardening to provide that year-round, organic food supply.

Once I became a more experienced gardener, I was able to adapt and learn new things about creating the ideal climate for my plants. Over time, my harvest became more and more predictable and plentiful. As my harvest grew, I began to explore other ways to use this experience to my advantage: I learned how to sell produce and profit from my hobby. You might be surprised how many people are willing to spend on produce they know is homegrown and pesticide-free!

Since then, I've been to other locations and climates as well, including the American Southwest. Once again, I had to adapt to an entirely new climate, and once again, I was able to use my greenhouse to provide the ideal environment for my garden. I'm delighted to say that I now have a consistent, year-round source of fresh, healthy food that I can enjoy and share with others.

## What is a Backyard Greenhouse?

Put simply, a backyard greenhouse is a smaller greenhouse than what you might see at a farm or nursery. Put a bit more descriptively, **a backyard greenhouse is a small structure made up of clear (usually plastic or glass) panels that help the owner regulate the climate to better grow plants**. Greenhouses are traditionally used to house and grow plants that need a warm environment to flourish.

The structure is usually in the silhouette of a house, but there are many different types of greenhouses. Smaller greenhouses may even look like ladders with plastic draped over them. Larger greenhouses may take up over 1,000 square feet and be equipped with electricity and an HVAC system. However your greenhouse looks, the purpose is to provide a home for your plants. If you do it right, this sealed system protects your plants from pests, disease, and adverse climates.

Greenhouses provide many benefits. They allow you to easily transplant seedlings and adult crops with a large degree of success; they give you a warm place to grow plants when the climate outside is dry or cold; they naturally provide a barrier to insects and pests like squirrels, rabbits, and mice; and they also provide a beautiful structure - depending on how you build it. In many cases, greenhouse owners use their greenhouses to add a visual appeal to their property.

But these structures also have some disadvantages, including the cost. Depending on the type of build you choose, a new greenhouse can be expensive. The larger the structure, the more expensive it can be to regulate the temperature through heating and ventilation. Along the same lines, a fully-functioning greenhouse can increase your electricity and water bills if you are not careful about regulating utilities. They also require an extra degree of work to monitor and maintain the structure and its resident plant life.

That being said, your greenhouse can look and operate however you choose. That's one of the beauties of greenhouse gardening - you can customize it however you want! This flexibility and allowance for creativity are some of the many reasons that people have grown to love this style of gardening.

But greenhouses have attracted enthusiasts with more than their flexibility and beauty. Greenhouses take the general benefits of gardening and amplify them. Not only do people become healthier physically, but mentally as well.

## Greenhouses Boost Your Health

### *Stress Relief*

The stress of day-to-day life affects us all and finding a hobby to help manage that stress can be extremely helpful. Those who have made gardening a hobby experience lower cortisol levels (our fight-or-flight hormone). When we're constantly stressed, those high cortisol levels can strain our body's systems and we begin to see physical symptoms like high blood pressure and heart disease.

A greenhouse takes all the relaxing benefits of gardening and gathers them up into a peaceful environment that you are able to change and adjust as you see fit. Even if the world around you is in chaos, your greenhouse can be a sanctuary.

## *Fitness and Exercise*

Anyone who's done any sort of gardening knows that it's not all just standing and holding a hose! An involved gardener is squatting, digging deep into the earth, pulling up weeds, and lifting bags of soil.

Even though there are a ton of varying movements in this hobby, they all occur at a relaxed pace. Even if you have mobility issues, joint pain, or difficulty putting strength into your limbs, you can still benefit from these low-intensity movements.

The best part is, if you wanted to, you could increase the intensity at any time. Just focus on using all your muscles when shoveling or move bags of soil into the greenhouse faster. This is a workout for any fitness level!

## *Sunlight and Vitamin D*

I know what the research says about UV rays, but sunlight is still one of the best sources of vitamin D for human beings! We need vitamin D for things like healthy bones. It stimulates enzymes to create vitamin D3, which eventually gets activated in the kidneys. This active form is what stimulates calcium reabsorption and eventually helps to reinforce our strong bones!

Too much health jargon? **Vitamin D = Strong Bones**. What better place to get lots of sunlight than your well-lit greenhouse? Experts say we should aim to get between 10-30 minutes of sun several times per week (although this can differ by person). You're practicing good health, just be spending time in your greenhouse! Just make sure to use appropriate sun protection such as sun block if you are spending lots of time outside.

## *Mental Health*

While you're working your physical muscles, your mental muscles are also in overdrive. Greenhouse gardening requires a lot of mindfulness, presence, and focus, not to mention problem-solving and critical thinking. All of these things are necessary to be successful. If you just stick something in the ground and hope it grows - well, you might get lucky. Chances are, you won't, and your crop will die.

Gardening tends to make us feel good as we care for something outside of ourselves. We get away from cluttered and stressful thinking and get to dwell on something we're building and nurturing. These positive thoughts release feel-good chemicals like serotonin and dopamine. Greenhouse gardening can provide a huge boost to your mood and mental processes.

## *Community*

There's something about food that brings people together, and that goes for whether we are serving it or growing it. When you get others involved with your greenhouse, you build deeper relationships. Working together for a common goal that can help solidify bonds. Inviting your kids, siblings, parents, or friends to join you in your greenhouse - even if you're not working - creates a memory and a moment that you share. As social beings, we need these moments with other people to refresh us and keep us from feeling isolated and alone.

# The Allure of the Harvest

As I mentioned above, greenhouse gardening attracts people for a lot of different reasons. But at the end of the day, people just want to grow the best possible crops they can, as much as they can.

Growing our own crops allows us to save money on buying food. With inflation going the way that it has over the last few years, people have begun researching and exploring self-sufficiency more than ever before. You can save a lot of money just by growing your own produce! This allows you to add a normally expensive grocery bill back into your bank account.

Another attractive feature is the fact that you no longer have to wait on whether or not grocery stores have the products you like in stock or on sale. You never have to go into the grocery store and wonder if a particular produce is in season. With the flexibility and the customization features of a greenhouse, you can grow whatever food you want, when you want. In addition, your success rate is much higher by using a greenhouse because you have greater control over the variables affecting your plants.

Of course, we've already mentioned that one of the greatest benefits to growing your produce is that you know what's in it. You know if your fruits and vegetables have been touched by pesticides or enhanced by hormones or other chemicals. As we'll outline in this book, you can grow fresh and plentiful produce without the use of artificial stimulants, repellents, or pesticides.

Lastly, there's something about growing your own food that just makes it taste so much better! Perhaps it's the fact that you were able to cultivate the soil and plant your produce in such a way that makes the flavor stand out. Or maybe it's just the taste of satisfaction and success, knowing that you have put in all of this work and finally seen the reward for your labor. Whatever it is, most people will readily admit that homegrown produce just tastes better.

As you create your greenhouse garden, you will no doubt learn new and wonderful lessons. You will see the results of your hard work and enjoy the rewards it produces. And somewhere along the way, you may even learn a little about yourself. Backyard-greenhouse owners get a unique perspective on gardening. As you read through this book, I hope you can adopt that perspective, too. This book will help you understand how to get started and take the right steps to grow a successful and plentiful garden - all while learning more about yourself in the process.

# Chapter 1:

# Preparing Yourself

As the renowned Benjamin Franklin once said, "...by failing to prepare, you are preparing to fail." To have a successful backyard greenhouse, we must practice the principle of preparation from the very beginning. Part of that preparation involves planning, gathering the materials, setting the layout, and educating ourselves on what it takes to set things in motion.

Life teaches us that we should always prepare ourselves for each new endeavor. Gardening is no different. Many different things go into the preparation and planning process. One of the first things we should do when planning out our greenhouse is to identify what the overall goal is. What are you looking for from your garden?

Are you looking to spend time participating in a healthy hobby? If so, then you may just need a smaller greenhouse with easy-to-care-for plants that allow you to experience all the joys of being a gardener without the hardship and struggle of more complex designs. Are you hoping to grow your own crops and be self-sustainable? If so, you'll need to gather the appropriate materials and plants, identify timelines for growth, and plan ahead for harvesting and storage to be ready for your ideal harvest. Are you growing crops for a business? Then you definitely need to identify timelines, coordinate marketing, arrange for services to be provided, and allow time for planting, growth, and harvesting.

You also need the right tools for the trade. Depending on how many plants you're growing, as well as how large your greenhouse is, the types of tools may differ. In this chapter, we'll go over a few of the basic tools that every gardener should have. However, that list is not exhaustive. Make sure to identify the tools you need as well as how to use them. If you have questions about how to solve a certain problem or you don't think the tool you currently have is working correctly, there are many veteran greenhouse gardeners online and in gardening groups who would be happy to share advice and information with you. You can also stop by your local plant nursery, where the staff is usually eager to help guide beginners on their garden journey.

You are already on the right track to educating yourself by reading this book. However, there may be other things you want to explore that are not covered here. Finding a variety of resources and networking with other people can help you develop the knowledge you need to better plan and implement your greenhouse garden.

Growing your knowledge and understanding will also mean keeping records and reviewing successes and failures to replicate them or make adjustments as necessary. As you read through this chapter, create a vision of your ideal greenhouse. If you need inspiration, there are thousands with a quick Pinterest search. You can even take it a step further and create a vision board. That vision will serve as the guiding force for your decisions and design.

## Choosing the Right Location

It's time to do a little scouting! Planning out where your greenhouse will be stationed is an important part of establishing your structure. To prepare for a productive greenhouse, you need to consider how you're going to use your greenhouse, how much space you have, and how much you'll need to accomplish your goal. This is where you set the foundation for your backyard homestead. The first thing is to contemplate the space that you'll be using for your greenhouse. Will you dedicate part of the backyard to this project? Will it be the whole backyard? Is a corner sufficient? Is the area between the fence and the house adequate? Do you need a large greenhouse or a small one?

Knowing the footprint of the greenhouse allows you to make smart and precise decisions about the size that you'll need. As a general rule, most prospective greenhouse owners should find the space they want to place their greenhouse and decide on a size that fills that space. This goes for those who want to start small as well. Often, people want to grow and expand their greenhouse after their first few harvests. Getting a larger greenhouse than you currently plan on using gives you the flexibility to grow your system however you'd like. It's always better to have too much space than too little.

You should also start planning what kind of crops you want to raise. Although we'll talk more about different kinds of vegetables you can plant in later chapters, having an idea of when you're going to start raising your crops can help you determine how you are going to prepare your space. Do you need shelving for small seedlings and other plants? Or are you going to fill the structure with raised garden beds?

Consider the location of the greenhouse in relation to other structures, trees, or other large sources of shade. Usually, greenhouses require sunlight to help drive up the temperature and create a warm environment in which the crops housed inside can thrive. However, it's important to note that depending on what kind of plants you're growing, you may not want them in direct sunlight. Finding a source of shade can help minimize how many times you need to intervene because of the sweltering heat in your structure. This is particularly important depending on the climate you live in. If you are in a particularly hot or desert climate, you will need to pay attention to the amount and intensity of sunlight provided.

Don't forget to note any local sources of pests or insects. If you have your greenhouse near a stagnant body of water, expect to see insects that hover there trying to invade your greenhouse. If you choose to plant near forests or other areas that make great animal dens, you'll eventually see a critter or two. Paying attention to the other creatures living in the area and planning for them can not only make your plants more comfortable, but you as well.

## Tools of the Trade

To start any gardening expedition, you'll need to collect the appropriate tools. If you've already been exploring the gardening scene, you probably have some of these tools already. Just in case, let's check out the basics.

## *Garden Spade*

Often confused with a "trowel", a **garden spade** is an essential tool for all gardeners. The garden spade generally refers to a short tool used to scoop dirt and move small plants. A spade is typically no more than 4 feet long and used for the cultivation and development of the landscape. It's basically a small shovel, though this tool has a design that makes it easier to move and use! Garden spade heads have a flattened shape with a square blade. The shape of the blade helps to dig deep planting holes as well as cut through grass and dirt to design and create space for new gardens.

There are several different types of spades and they can all be used in many different ways. The general use for a garden spade is to move soil and cultivate garden beds. But spades can also be used to move plants around and form clear-cut borders and edges. Due to its shape, the spade is easier to manipulate than shovels or other digging tools. The spade's design provides great leverage for sharp and quick movements, like digging up dense weeds or grass.

Make sure to care for your spade, and it will take care of you. Keeping the edges sharp ensures that it continues to make quick and precise cuts for your garden beds. If you plan on gardening for the foreseeable future, make sure to invest in a spade that will be sturdy enough to hold up to the test of time. Steel or carbon make great materials for a strong and durable blade.

## *Garden Trowel*

A typical **garden trowel** is a small, versatile, handheld shovel. Often confused with the garden spade, a trowel is much shorter and has a different purpose. The shovel portion is typically either metal or plastic and has a short, easy-to-wield handle. This tool can be used to create small holes to plant bulbs or create space for transplanting both seedlings and mature crops. The trowel is normally used for smaller plants, as it would take a lot of time and energy to dig large holes for bigger vegetation like trees or bushes. They also make a great tool for pulling up weeds and scooping soil to fill small holes or pots.

There are several different types of trowels: some are short and wide and may be used for removing weeds, while others are longer and narrower to help you transplant young vegetation to their new home. If you are in doubt about which kind of trowel to purchase, it's best to go with a basic one you can find at any local garden store, as it can be used for any purpose.

## *Garden Shears*

You'll be doing a lot of trimming and pruning as you care for your plants, so **garden shears** are another essential tool for a backyard gardener! There are two main kinds of shears: bypass shears are the most common tools that gardeners will use, usually when pruning their plants; and anvil shears, which are less common and require a better knowledge of how to cut branches and stems effectively.

Garden shears allow you to create clean cuts and deftly maneuver around plants. They are sharpened scissors that can slice through thick stems, while still being versatile enough to navigate small areas and spaces. The type of garden shears that you use should allow you to create space for the healthy regrowth of your fruits and vegetables.

As a note, make sure that the shears you choose fit your hands well. You can have a really great blade, but if you are unable to fit your hand around the handles or if you have a weaker grip, you may have difficulty using the shears for longer periods of time. Look for something comfortable that will help to provide the cutting leverage needed to do the job.

Shears can go a long way if you take good care of them. That includes keeping them away from any water or other liquid that could cause rust and corrosion. Proper care also means cleaning them regularly and wiping off any particles, soil, or plant residue after use.

## *Gardening Gloves*

I know, I know! What's probably coming to your mind right now is a dainty little pair of yellow, flowery cloth gloves. People often take safety for granted and don't consider protective gear until after we run into medical problems. Take it from me, one of the most important tools you can invest in is a quality pair of **gardening gloves**!

I don't care how tough your hands are, if you truly want to create a thriving and effective greenhouse environment, you'll be putting in a lot of work that can be damaging to your hands in the long term. Even if you are not getting injuries every day, the strain that you put on your hands can have compounding effects later in life.

A good pair of gloves will protect your hands from cuts, abrasions, punctures, blisters, and splinters, but that's not all. A good pair of gloves can help you to get a secure grip and increase the power that you put into using your tools. The more leverage and grip you can have on your tools, the less strain you are putting on your wrists and other muscles as you work. This can decrease the risks of arthritis, sprains, and muscle strain over time. If you want to make this a thriving business and a long-term hobby, you'll need to ensure that you can keep going as well. Take care of yourself. Buy some high-quality gardening gloves.

Make sure to select gloves based on durability and their ability to handle difficult jobs. You'll want something that can breathe and help decrease the heat and sweat which collects from your skin, but also that can protect against chemicals, insect bites, and any fungus or infections you may find in your plants.

Every glove has pros and cons to its use. What's most important is that you figure out what you want to use your gloves for (i.e. what kind of gardening you are planning on doing) and what feels the most comfortable to you. The best gardeners will have multiple gloves that serve different purposes. Leather gloves are both durable and waterproof and provide great natural protection; cloth gloves are breathable and easy to work in but provide less protection, neoprene or rubber gloves are great for protecting hands from chemicals as well as any cuts and scrapes and are good for when you know you'll be dealing with plants that may have infections.

Choose your gloves wisely, and you'll be able to handle any situation that may arise. Don't take this garden tool lightly!

## *Optional Tools*

Some tools are less common for backyard greenhouse gardening. These tools are often used for larger farming endeavors, however, depending on how you design your backyard garden, can still come in handy.

**Some less essential tools that can still be helpful in your greenhouse venture include hoes, garden forks, and wheelbarrows.** Hoes are generally useful for dealing with weeds and cultivating the soil. They make it easier to stir up the soil and aerate it. You can also use them to break through and loosen up weeds to make them easier to remove.

Garden forks are useful for breaking up dirt and stirring the soil to mix compost and other helpful additives. They also help with transporting plants that you plan on turning over or mulching later.

Wheelbarrows are useful in transportation as well as temporary storage solutions. If you need to move and store soil in a particular area while you try to fill in part of your garden, a wheelbarrow provides a great mobile solution.

# What to Expect

As we begin this journey, start preparing yourself for a marathon. Many people go into gardening thinking they can put some seeds in the ground and begin harvesting big, fresh crops just a few weeks later. That sounds great, but that's not how it works.

Caring for plants requires a lot of time and effort, especially if you want them to produce a bountiful harvest. You'll be constantly monitoring temperatures, moisture, and plant health, as well as many other factors to make sure that your greenhouse environment is optimal.

Gardening is an art form. Greenhouse gardening is no different. Prepare to practice some patience, determination, and self-forgiveness (you will make mistakes). But any setbacks or challenges you face will pale in comparison to the rewarding experience of watching that first seedling sprout.

Consider keeping a journal to document all the progress that you've made. It allows you to look back and reflect on the things that were successful and the things that were not. Journaling also allows you to set a baseline for what to expect in the future. You can look at all the different things that you've learned and set new expectations so that you can respond and plan appropriately for whatever your next steps are.

## Chapter 2:

# Designing the Greenhouse

This chapter is going to be a little more detailed and complex. After all, how you design your greenhouse can dictate what kind of plants you can grow, as well as how much and how efficiently. Even after you read all of the information in this chapter, remember that there is still so much more that you can learn. Try tweaking different designs until they best suit your purposes. Use this information as a baseline and continue to grow and adapt as your vision demands.

Before making any decisions about the type of greenhouse you are going to install, make sure you are aware of any county restrictions. Your greenhouse is going to be another structure on your property and learning about restrictions or regulations involving additional structures can help to avoid future problems. Check your county and HOA policies and keep those limitations in mind when designing your greenhouse.

As part of your preparation process, you should've determined the location of your greenhouse already. This means that you know if it's going to be close to your residence, or further away. After you have determined the location of your greenhouse, it's time to determine what type of greenhouse you need.

I could fill several books with instructions on how to put together different greenhouse designs. Yes, there are that many! There's just not enough room to cover them all. But there are plenty of resources online that provide detailed guides for constructing your greenhouse. I recommend you start with well-known home improvement/gardening companies. In fact, both Home Depot and Lowes have very detailed online guides for building greenhouses, from laying the foundation to ideas for customization.

## Types of Greenhouses

While attached and freestanding greenhouses are the two most well-known and common types of greenhouses, there are several sub-types under each of these.

### *Cold Frame*

The easiest way to tell the difference between a **cold frame** and a traditional greenhouse is that a cold frame does not come with electric, heating, or ventilation systems. A cold frame is a structure in which the heating is provided by the sun's rays.

These rays will heat up the building, which insulates and provides the warm climate needed for plants to grow.

Typically, cold frame greenhouses are used for plants that may be outside of their typical climate or season. This works especially well for cold season plants that are more hearty and able to handle cold night temperatures. These include broccoli, kale, peas, radishes, carrots, and many others. In fact, cold frame greenhouses are often used by commercial and agricultural growers to extend their growing season.

These frames can also be used by backyard growers, but they are usually much smaller and they are kept in places where weather is more unpredictable. Cold frames are ideal for starting seeds. They can also help keep tropical plants safe over the winter and fall seasons. This is done by inducing a dormant state so that they will be ready to continue growing after the final frost before spring.

There are many different kinds of cold frames and you will have to determine which one is best for your space and your needs. Some cold frame designs include **sunken cold frames**, in which a pit is created for plants to sit in and then covered with either rigid plastic or glass. Another type is a typical hoop tunnel frame, which is supported by a series of arches creating a **tunnel-shaped** greenhouse and is often used by agricultural farmers. This cold frame helps to keep the soil warm and protects sensitive plants during the cool season. Then there is the cold frame that only stands a few feet tall and is basically a box with glass or rigid plastic pulled over it. Usually, this is a portable wooden frame and allows gardeners to provide a place for hardening off young plants.

## *Attached*

An **attached greenhouse** has four sides but shares one weight-bearing wall with another structure. Usually, people will use their garage, a shed, or their own house. The benefit of this design is that you won't need to build all the walls since you share with another building, and that means you don't have to invest as much in the other three greenhouse walls. Attached greenhouses are generally less expensive than standalone greenhouses. Sometimes you can share the heating bill with the structure that they are attached to, and they don't require any extra paths or structures that you might see in a freestanding greenhouse.

The downside is that attached greenhouses are designed and dictated by the structure you are using for its attachment. That environment can be harder to control because it can be influenced by the environment of the structure it is attached to. For example, if the attached greenhouse is connected to your home, your home's temperature could influence the temperature of the greenhouse.

One of the most common greenhouses for this subtype is the **lean-to greenhouse**. Usually, it's set up to lean against a structure like a wall or side of the house. You can also put it up against garages and sheds. This is a pretty simple greenhouse to maintain, and it is also easy to heat because the structure can use the heat from the building that it is up against.

A less common type of attached greenhouse is the **even-span greenhouse**. This is very similar to the lean-to but it does not lean against the house. Instead, it stands flush against the house. Again, this version is cheaper to heat because the wall is shared with the building, so it receives some of the heat that the building produces. This greenhouse gives you all the space for plant growth as a freestanding greenhouse but still gives you all the same benefits as a lean-to.

As a separate note, there are also **uneven-span greenhouses**. These are very uncommon; however, you'll see them in places where the ground may be disjointed and require some more creative structuring in order to make a greenhouse work. Like the lean-to and even-span, they are still attached to the home, shed, garage, or other structure in some way.

An attached greenhouse may seem like a pretty neat idea but there are downsides. The first and most obvious is that you will have to deal with the shadow of the structure you are leaning up against for part of the day. Unless the greenhouse is located on the south facing wall of the structure (north, if you are in the southern hemisphere), the sun will eventually fall behind the structure and the greenhouse as the earth rotates. If you don't preemptively plan for this, it can really mess up your design plans. Another downside is the inability to fully control every aspect of your climate in the greenhouse. Because the climate of the greenhouse will be significantly influenced by the climate of the structure it's snuggled up to, you may have some difficulty trying to set a very specific temperature or trying to adjust the natural temperature of the two buildings.

## *Freestanding*

On the other hand, a **freestanding greenhouse** allows you the flexibility to design your greenhouse and structure it however you want. You can create a completely new space with very few restrictions! Freestanding greenhouses also allow you a much larger space to accommodate and grow more plants.

You can create various layouts and even create a small sitting area if you wish. Imagine creating your own little oasis of peace, far away from the distractions of daily living, a place where you can freely escape for an hour or two every day. Freestanding greenhouses can serve as that relaxing and tranquil location, away from the hustle and bustle of the office and the responsibilities of home life.

Although this is a beautiful possibility, you should know that these structures tend to be more expensive and will require extra time and energy to both install and maintain. Freestanding greenhouses come with a higher price tag because they need to be made of better materials in order to be sturdy and durable enough to stand on their own.

Freestanding greenhouses come in many different forms, just like attached greenhouses. Freestanding greenhouses provide more space because they have their own walls, roofs, and floor. These greenhouses are great if you have space and require more room for your plants to grow. These also have their own even-span models.

**Even-span greenhouses** are the most common type of freestanding greenhouses. They are usually characterized by their pointed roofs and standard "house" look. Greenhouse users love them because they let in tons of sunlight and give off a spacious feel.

Other greenhouses found in this category include **A-frames** and **gothic arch greenhouses.** These are less common and can come in a variety of different designs and materials, but they still stand on their own as separate structures.

# Building a Greenhouse

Building your own greenhouse can be a very fun and inexpensive way to create a home for your crops. However, it can also be tedious and will take a lot of effort to plan. Deciding on the greenhouse design you're going to construct is the first hurdle you'll have to cross. Although you have a lot of flexibility in design, there are basic structures that work best and have been used time and time again. Make sure to research various greenhouse designs to determine which one works best for your space as well as your needs.

There are many greenhouses that come in specialized kits that make it easy for people to install - much like putting up a camping tent! These kits are usually pretty standard, so if you want something customized or to have more control over the type of materials you use, you may want to add and remove things from these kits or build the entire greenhouse from scratch yourself.

## *Flooring*

Generally, most people like using **concrete** floors for their greenhouse. This provides a solid foundation and also offer the option of watering it down in order to increase humidity and retain heat throughout the day. Concrete is also much easier to clean and maintain over a long period of time. **Bricks or pavers** can also be laid down in a beautiful design that will add to the charm of your greenhouse.

If you're looking for something more aesthetically pleasing, consider **landscape or lava rock**. These come in many different shapes, sizes, and colors. They are not as easy to clean, but they do help to maintain humidity in the greenhouse.

Just like normal gardens, **landscape fabric or weed mats** make good coverings for the ground. They help keep weeds out of the greenhouse, are easy to install, and are typically inexpensive. Depending on the kinds you purchase, it can be harder to clean, so take that into account when considering this option. Some gardeners put gravel over the top of the fabric, which helps keep it in place, making it a practical design choice.

As building materials have developed and evolved over time, many materials that have traditionally been used in residential homes are now being explored as options for greenhouses, including vinyl tiles. This type of flooring is more expensive, but when installed in a greenhouse, they clean easily and drain well. Not to mention, they look beautiful!

## *Windows*

When it comes to windows, make sure you spend adequate time considering your options. After all, windows are a huge part of what makes a greenhouse a greenhouse! Contrary to what you might think, greenhouse windows are not always made of glass. However, glass is the best quality and will last the longest out of any other material that you can use for a greenhouse window.

**Tempered glass** is the preferred type of glass for most greenhouses. This material is sturdy and resistant to shattering. If these windows do shatter, they break into chunks that are safer than the jagged strips other forms of glass might produce. Additionally, you can always find double-tempered glass which increases the strength and shatter-resistance.

Yes, glass is pretty impressive and looks great, but you do pay for it. Glass is expensive and putting in multiple panels of glass can easily hike up the cost of your greenhouse, especially if you are trying to get better-quality glass windows. This could be an area where you consider the eco-friendly option of purchasing second hand or antique windows that can be repurposed for the greenhouse. You will save tons of money going this route if you consider yourself to be handy and are willing to patiently gather the supplies. If you're less inclined to go on a treasure hunt in the name of being eco-friendly or cutting expenses, you may want to consider some other options.

Other types of greenhouse window materials include **polycarbonate**, which is more affordable, lightweight, and easier to manipulate. These are some of the best alternatives to glass windows and have some of the same aesthetic appeal. Polycarbonate windows can even be altered to have automatic openers, just like glass windows. This allows you to control the climate of the greenhouse much more easily. One downside to polycarbonate, though, is that it degrades over time after being exposed to UV light. This can cause ugly splotches to begin to appear on the windows.

**Polyethylene or polyfilm sheeting** comes in different thicknesses and opacity. Polyfilm is essentially a plastic sheeting that covers the frame of your greenhouse. This window/shade type is generally good as an inexpensive option for short-term use. It's not nearly as durable as either polycarbonate or glass, but it does do well with insulation and helps to keep heat within the greenhouse. Unfortunately, it does make ventilation and air circulation more difficult.

Greenhouse windows should also have **frames**. Frames often come in either **vinyl or aluminum**. While aluminum is lighter, it allows for more heat loss in greenhouses. Vinyl is heavier and more expensive but seems to be better at preventing condensation buildup and heat loss. Either way, your windows should fit into your opening securely in order to prevent the climate outside from influencing the climate inside your greenhouse.

During this whole process, make sure you are asking the important questions. Windows are arguably one of the most important decisions to building a greenhouse, and you don't want to skimp on them. Speak with professionals and make sure you have all the information you need before you purchase your windows/covering.

## *Location*

Again, we need to come back to the location. Location deserves this extra emphasis because it is extremely important when building your own greenhouse. Where you plan to build your greenhouse should be decided based on what you plan to grow in the greenhouse and what kind of greenhouse you plan to build. You may have plants that require equal amounts of shade and sun, or more of one or the other. **For most people living in the northern hemisphere, it's best to build your greenhouse so you get the most out of the sunlight coming from the south. That's where the bulk of your sunlight comes from. Therefore, the length of your greenhouse should be from the east to the west.**

Pay attention to the direction of the sun and the intensity. As we explore later on in these chapters, some plants love heat, but not too much heat. Some like lots of heat, but not direct sunlight. You may also need to consider everyday risks like storms, local wildlife, and even other people. For example, you probably don't want to build a greenhouse in an area that's known for flooding - or right across from a golf course.

Account for any water, electricity, or sources of heating that you may need for your greenhouse. If you're considering a lean-to, you might be able to account for some of the heat being produced from your home. You'll likely hike up your energy bill, but you may save money instead of just heating the greenhouse separately.

Keep in mind the condition of the ground where you build your greenhouse. **Avoid building a greenhouse on a slope or where water flows downhill.** You want the ground to be well-draining so that standing water won't collect. Inspect your prospective land beforehand, paying close attention to the ground and making sure the area is level and flat. This could also help you avoid the cost of having to level the ground before you can establish your greenhouse.

Don't forget to include space for expansion in case you decide to grow your greenhouse or add another one. Keep the surrounding area in mind! Make a note of whether the area around your greenhouse space contains lots of pests or if it is close to other native plants or plants being grown by neighbors. If those native or neighbor plants get infected with a disease, you don't want those transmitted to your crops. This should all be taken into consideration when deciding where to build a greenhouse.

## Buying a Greenhouse

If you're going to buy a quality greenhouse, you should be prepared to spend a hefty sum of money. That said, it's important to note that smaller and lower-quality greenhouses have now become more affordable for those who want to try the experience first without fully committing. A full commitment requires a quality greenhouse, however, and that's not cheap.

When buying a greenhouse, once again consider the size of the greenhouse that you want to buy. Are you trying to purchase a starter greenhouse with just enough space for a bench and a small garden bed? Or are you trying to get something much larger that will require space and effort to install?

Oh, yes! Even if you buy a greenhouse, there is still some assembly required – unless you have someone do it for you. Here seems like a good place to reiterate that you should get more greenhouse than you think you will need, money permitting. This gives you room to grow as you get more and more accustomed to the process of gardening and managing a greenhouse.

Just like with building a greenhouse from scratch, you also have to decide what kind of panels you want for your greenhouse. Glass, polycarbonate, and polyethylene all vary widely in cost, with polyethylene being the most affordable. Likewise, consider the materials that make up the frame. Whether you're using plastic, aluminum, wood, or some form of metal, you will be paying premium prices. At the time of this writing, the cost of lumber is at a high, so frames that have wood as their base may prove more expensive than other options. Plastic is an inexpensive and lightweight alternative. Most designs have a plastic frame that is easy to install.

As usual, make sure that you understand any regulations that your neighborhood might have as well as any zoning laws that your county may have. Since you'll be installing a kit all at once, you won't have a lot of space to level the ground or do other alterations once the structure is set up. Your ability to customize the greenhouse based on location will also be very limited. You won't be able to make any alterations to the greenhouse design you're given, so you want to make sure that your location has been optimized for success.

There are many different greenhouses for sale on the market. Some come from reputable companies, while others are from private sellers. Most greenhouses worth your time will cost some money and will require time and effort to install. Be wary of people who make it seem as though their product is too good to be true, because it just might be.

Read up on the company that you're buying from and understand their policies, including warranty and shipping. If the greenhouse you're interested in is a bit complex, you may also want to look into whether or not they offer customer service or technical assistance. That way, you have people that you can ask about the structural design.

Getting to know other backyard greenhouse owners provides you with helpful connections, too. Find out what they've heard and what they use for their products. If you know people in your neighborhood, see what they are up to. You can also join a gardening society and learn some of the local and online products they use. Alternatively, you can check online gardening forums. Many of the gardeners on online forums are happy to share their experiences and give advice.

## Accessories to Consider

For any greenhouse, bought or built, there are several accessories your plants can benefit from. While these are not *essential* for any greenhouse, they are certainly *helpful*.

### *Thermometers*

I know that we often think about greenhouses as a way to help plants keep warm from the cold, but without properly managing temperature, we can risk heating plants too much, too. Plants that are sensitive to heat may wilt and burn. Heat can also build in locations with stale air, as well as increase the humidity in the space. Increases in humidity can attract pests and make your plants more susceptible to disease.

Using a thermometer will allow you to monitor the temperature of your greenhouse at any time. The more accurate the device, the better you can establish your climate. When considering thermometers, there are many different kinds, especially in the era of advanced technology. Do your due diligence to determine which kind of thermometer is within your price range and will meet your needs.

Digital thermometers can be very useful because they are easy to read. In addition, a lot of digital thermometers now come with hygrometers so that you can also monitor the water vapor in the air and measure the humidity. This is a pretty useful tool for a greenhouse environment.

If you're feeling particularly ambitious, you can explore the idea of a greenhouse weather station. These devices monitor the climate inside your greenhouse as well as outside. The most advanced versions can even tell you how the elements on the outside will influence your greenhouse climate so you can make preparations and plan for changes in weather accordingly. For many people, this may be seen as an excessive purchase, and for many people it is. But if you have the funds, or you desire absolute precision, it is a pretty neat tool.

## *Ventilation*

**Ventilation may be one of the most important aspects of greenhouse development.** Not only does ventilation help you prevent moisture accumulation in the greenhouse – which can lead to disease – it also helps you keep pests in and out of your environment. It also assists in temperature control, a very important factor for manually maintaining your greenhouse. Whether your greenhouse is a cold frame and heated by the sun, or electrically heated, ventilation will be necessary in order to meet the needs of your crops.

Good ventilation should allow your plants to get plenty of the carbon dioxide they need in order to photosynthesize. There should also be some kind of circulation unit, whether it be a fan or an industrial circulator to help move the air around, so that all of the plants get the air needed.

Ventilation is also important because it can help create an atmosphere that crop-damaging insects will not find ideal. Insects like to be comfortable, and if their environment is constantly changing and being disturbed (for example, with a wind consistently blowing through the area), then they are less likely to stick around.

There are several different types of vents and fans that you can buy to help meet your needs. Many models come with basic roof vents for greenhouses. Depending on your style of greenhouse, you may need to add more vents. If you have a larger and more developed greenhouse, you can add solar vents that open and close based on the temperature in the greenhouse. Every greenhouse should have at least one vent near the roof of the greenhouse so that rising heat can escape and fresh air can find its way inside. Alternatively, you can have multiple vents around the perimeter that can help capture more wind and also allow more air to flow out. These vents should be able to be closed in the event that you need to change the temperature or climate in the greenhouse. As mentioned before, sometimes exhaust fans can help to circulate the air efficiently so that your plants can be well pollinated, as well as exposed to air.

## *Shelving and Storage*

Shelving and storage are essential for an efficient greenhouse. Most greenhouse owners attach their shelving on the inside with careful planning to make sure that space is used effectively. Shelving benches, pots, and other structures can help provide better placement and space for plants. These also help you maintain proper access to all the different things that you'll need to use throughout your gardening career.

**When installing shelving, it should be at a height that works for you or anyone who is going to be spending time in the greenhouse.** Many people, in their haste to increase storage, have put shelves at heights that were too high. Storage can become inconvenient if your shelves are too high and safety can become a concern. Others have put shelves much too low, making it inconvenient to put anything down there, or inaccessible to gardeners with joint or mobility problems.

Proper shelving should be comfortable and should not get in the way of your daily usage. Since you'll be spending a lot of time in your greenhouse, you want to make sure that you are comfortable while you are there.

# The Right Greenhouse for You

With all of these different options, it's been overwhelming to think about which is the best greenhouse. The truth is, you don't have to find the very best greenhouse, you don't have to look for the greenhouse that has all the nice bells and whistles, you just have to decide on the greenhouse that is best for you. Think about where you want to put your greenhouse, the kinds of plants that you want to grow, and the overall space that you are trying to develop. That will dictate what kind of greenhouse is best for you.

As you consider each factor and think about the type of space that you're trying to fill, this information will help you select the right greenhouse.

For example, let's say that you decide you want a small garden, so you decide to go with a medium sized greenhouse. But it's kind of an awkward space that you're trying to fill. You don't want it leaning up against any structures, so you know it needs to stand alone. You've got some extra cash on hand, so you opt to buy rather than build.

You order a rectangular 4x6 freestanding greenhouse. The structure seems to sit well, and it looks nice in your existing landscape. You decide to save a little money for some extra crops and forgo the automatic ventilation, choosing to have manual vents instead. Knowing that you want to grow more tropical plants and, thus, need more humidity, you opt for a concrete floor that you can wet regularly to add to the humidity in the greenhouse.

You decide that your greenhouse should have double-tempered glass since it's safer and you have children and want to share with them the joys of gardening. Finally, you determine that staying within budget is most important and opt for the aluminum framing solution.

Now you have your ideal greenhouse and you're able to move forward into the next step of your greenhouse experience: choosing your plants!

**Chapter 3:**

# Picking Your Produce

You can grow almost anything in a greenhouse. After all, the whole purpose of a greenhouse is so you can have greater control over the climate surrounding your crops! But there are certain fruits that adapt more naturally to the native greenhouse environment than others.

Most of the following plants thrive in the warm, humid environments that greenhouses naturally provide. But keep in mind that, with some work, you can manipulate the environment to fit whatever setting you'd like.

In this chapter, I'll share a few common plants that you can explore to get started on your greenhouse journey.

# Some Fruity Options

## *Strawberries*

**Strawberries** make excellent fruits to plant in your greenhouse since they often struggle with the challenges of adjusting to climate change. Greenhouses allow you to control that climate as needed. Strawberries are also susceptible to many different kinds of pests, and a greenhouse provides some protection from these attackers. As far as consumption goes, strawberries are also a very popular fruit, and you'll always have a demand for strawberries, whether it be on your own table or in the market.

When planting your strawberries, consider using soil with high concentrations of organic matter. The optimal pH range should be between 5.5 and 7.0. You'll also want to make sure that the soil is well-draining and that you have mulch or straw to help keep roots from becoming too warm or exposed to the moisture always present in greenhouse air.

Strawberries love sunlight and need at least six hours of light every day, if not more. They make prime candidates for the part of your greenhouse that gets direct sun, so keep those windows clean and the space open for your strawberries! Along the same lines, it's important to note that strawberries like to flower in a very specific temperature range. Higher temperatures can impair growth and potentially kill the plant. The temperature should probably not go over 77°F; in fact, 60°F to 70°F is the optimal temperature.

Strawberries like to be watered regularly. However, they cannot survive in deep, waterlogged conditions. They will rot! This is why well-draining soil is important. Try to water from the base and give about an inch and a half of water each time. Irrigation can be very helpful for strawberry cultivation since these plants have shallow roots.

Strawberries require regular pruning and monitoring. During the first part of their growth, flowers will begin to blossom. Make sure to pinch those off, so the plants do not fruit too early or put energy into creating too many immature fruits. Doing this helps to ensure that it is transporting its nourishment to healthy and substantial fruit.

## *Bananas*

**Bananas**? In a greenhouse? I know it sounds crazy, but this next fruit is proof that anything is possible with a greenhouse. If you want to grow banana plants, you'll need to be very patient. Bananas take their time to grow.

Most everyone knows that bananas are tropical fruits, so by now I'm sure you realize that they are going to need to be kept warm and humid. Often, they produce multiple harvests and can take up a lot of space, so make sure to plan that space out beforehand.

There are many different varieties of banana plants. Make sure to know which kind of banana plant you are purchasing and attempting to grow. For most people, dwarf banana plants make better options than traditional, larger bananas, as these don't require as much space.

When planting your banana tree, you can either get one that is young or grow one from suckers (shoots) growing from the base of the stem. This also makes further propagation much easier. You can slice off one of the suckers and replant them in another location.

Banana trees will need heat over 70°F in order to grow and develop. These are plants that continue to thrive even when temperatures exceed 80°F or 90°F. Plan on keeping a hot and humid greenhouse when trying to grow banana plants. They need a lot of access to water! However, they don't like being flooded, which means developing a regular watering schedule is necessary to help them thrive.

Bananas require well-draining soil. There should also be plenty of organic content, as bananas are heavy feeders. A balance of soil and fertilizer can help satisfy their hunger. The soil should be kept somewhere between a pH of 6.0 and 7.0 and be kept moist.

At the end of its life cycle, a banana tree will give off shoots, which can steal nutrients from the main tree. You'll need to prune those shoots regularly. Bananas have a very specific lifecycle. After a banana plant fruits, it dies, and those shoots take over and begin a new tree. Make sure to save those shoots if you want to keep planting bananas!

## *Peaches*

**Peach** trees, while also not as common, are absolutely an option for greenhouse gardeners. They are slightly higher maintenance, as they require deep soil and are very sensitive to poor drainage. Roots can easily die when sitting for too long in water. The soil should be at a pH of around 6.5 and loamy.

Peaches are more ideal for your lean-to or cold frame greenhouse because they require a cold period in order to go dormant and accumulate "chilling hours". If they have enough chilling hours, the leaves, buds, and eventually fruit will develop with no problems. However, with too few chilling hours, the tree may develop problems including reduced fruit and delayed flowering. Thus, this fruit should probably not be growing with your warmer plants.

Peach trees require regular watering in order to make sure that the soil is kept moist, as well as in close contact with the tree roots. Some people also choose to train their trees: they tie off the shoots with training wires so that the tree opens in a fanned out shape. They also may trim the tree in order to help the root quality and prevent branches from snapping.

## *Oranges*

Just like bananas, you may want to consider a dwarf tree for growing **oranges,** or any kind of citrus for that matter. Also, much like bananas, orange trees will require a lot of heat and water. Keeping temperatures above 70°F is ideal; however, you can allow them to drop a little bit at night. During the winter, you will need to take extra care to protect them during a frost. Monitor the weather and if necessary, provide extra insulation like a frost cloth (essentially a winter coat for plants). Oranges require a lot of soil drainage but should be well-watered.

Oranges prefer a soil with a pH of around 6.0 to 7.5. The soil should be fertilized and kept moist, but not soaked. Allow the soil to dry a bit between waterings to encourage the uptake of nutrients. While the soil should not be kept exceptionally damp, orange trees still enjoy a good misting from a spray bottle every now and then.

Oranges also produce suckers and offshoots and these can be used to propagate new orange trees. This also means that the tree will require regular monitoring and pruning to make sure nutrition is not going towards the offshoots and is remaining focused on the main plant.

# Growing Your Veggies

Many vegetables have different requirements than fruits. Understanding these differences and preparing your greenhouse accordingly can help you successfully raise your veggies to maturity. Here are a few of the most common vegetables that backyard growers like to produce:

## *Corn*

I know, **corn** is not normally a vegetable you think you would find in a greenhouse. But, by now I hope you are beginning to understand that anything is possible! Corn is a staple for many diets and can be prepared in so many different ways that it will always be a popular vegetable.

Corn likes moist and well-drained soil. The soil pH is usually between 5.8 and 6.8. This soil should also have moderate levels of phosphorus and potassium and be above 60°F. Corn loves sandy, loamy soil, and you can enrich that soil with compost and other supplements to provide extra nutrients.

Watering for corn is rather simple. It needs lots of water, especially once it is germinated, and continuously throughout the growth cycle. Usually, corn can survive and do well on about an inch of water every two weeks.

Corn also requires lots of sunlight. This is one of the vegetables that you want to put in an area where the greenhouse receives the most sunlight. If your corn is not getting enough sun, you should supplement using grow lights. Speaking of finding space, **this crop is going to need a large area to grow and develop**! This is not a plant that can be grown in a small greenhouse. You'll need a medium- to large-sized greenhouse to accommodate this veggie.

## *Cucumbers*

There are many different kinds of **cucumbers** that can grow in a greenhouse. They do well in greenhouses because they love the warmth and heat! The good thing is that cucumbers don't take long to grow, and you can enjoy them pretty quickly after planting. If growing on a trellis, they tend to grow even bigger with even more shoots.

Cucumbers do well in soil that has a pH of around 6.0 to 7.0. The soil should be moist, but not waterlogged. When watering cucumbers, they will need small amounts administered often. After the plants have emerged further, they will require about a gallon of water per week.

Cucumbers are another vegetable that love sunlight and your greenhouse should be angled in such a way to help them receive at least six hours of sun. Cucumbers tend to mature and produce fruit quickly and will be ready for harvest in as little as 12 weeks.

## *Root Vegetables (carrots, potatoes, etc.)*

**Root vegetables** can be somewhat tricky because you can't see them: they grow underneath the ground! Some grow fast like radishes, while others take much longer to develop and mature, like carrots. Root vegetables are anything that bears the "fruit"

of the plant underground. While we mainly focus on the root portion of the plant, you can also eat the leafy greens of the plants as well.

Most root vegetables are planted as seeds and can quickly sprout into seedlings. At this point, they should be thinned out as they begin to sprout and grow their first leaves. That means that some plants need to be removed from the ground so that others have space to grow.

**Root vegetables need deep, well-draining soil.** The larger the root vegetable, the deeper the soil should be. Unlike other crops, these don't require rich soil and can grow in any basic soil composition. They do require phosphorus and potassium for healthy growth, though.

Root vegetables also require sunlight, although not as much as some of the more heat-loving vegetables. In fact, root vegetables prefer cool weather rather than heat. These vegetables also like to be watered consistently and don't do well when they experience seasons of low to no watering.

In most cases, root vegetables prefer to be sown directly into the soil and not grown as seedlings and then transplanted into the soil. Often, transplanting seedlings this way can damage the vegetable as it is pulled from the ground and then put back into the ground.

The time it takes from seed to harvest can vary for every root vegetable. Root vegetables can be grown in any season and some grow better or taste better during one particular season than another. Getting to know your vegetables will help you know when to plant them and how to time them.

## *Leafy Vegetables (Kale, Lettuce, etc.)*

Greenhouses provide **leafy vegetables** the opportunity to grow in their ideal climate. Most greens, however, enjoy cooler temperatures. You will need to organize your greenhouse in such a way to provide them just enough sun without letting them get too hot. These high temperatures will slow growth and development. Ideal temperatures are around 60°F to 65°F during the day.

Leafy vegetables generally enjoy soil that is loose and well-drained. The ideal pH of the soil should be around 5.0 to 6.0. It should also contain plenty of organic matter. As a note, this is one type of vegetable that can actually be grown hydroponically, meaning that you can grow many leafy greens without soil altogether. In a greenhouse, you would need to set up a hydroponic system to make sure that the plants get adequate nutrients from the water.

For most leafy vegetables, the growth rate slows during the winter and most of the growth and development happens during the warmer months. However, in a greenhouse, you can alter the climate so that they are consistently producing year-round. Just keep light intensity low to mimic a shaded light if that is the method used to provide sunlight to the plant.

## Herbaceous Tenants

Herbs are an entire learning experience unto themselves. Many people like to start with herbs to get the hang of gardening because they provide a good introduction to understanding plant differences. Herbs are generally easy to plant and grow and require minimal intervention. You can even grow them hydroponically if you set up the appropriate equipment in your greenhouse.

### *Rosemary*

Everybody loves **rosemary**: it's a beautiful plant that provides a lovely scent and delicious seasoning to any dish. However, unlike other herbs on this list, it prefers drier soil. You'll still need to keep it watered, but the soil should be well-drained and never waterlogged. Maintaining a soil pH of 6.0 to 7.0 is also a good idea. However, rosemary will do great in most soils and doesn't require much extra organic matter.

**This is one plant that needs to be trimmed often**, especially after the first flowering so that it becomes bushier and fuller. Make sure that this plant has plenty of sunlight, too, around six to eight hours. That being said, rosemary can also deal with partial shade if it needs to. Make sure this herb has adequate spacing so that the roots can spread out.

Rosemary can be started from both seeds and cuttings. Seeds can sometimes have a difficult time germinating and can be soaked to prime them for sprouting. Cuttings should ideally be dipped in a growth hormone before planting so they can take to the soil better.

One of the added benefits of rosemary is that it is a natural insect repellent. In fact, many people like to make their own homemade concoctions that can spread on their skin to protect them from unwanted pests. Some of the pests that rosemary deters include mosquitos, moths, flies, snails, and carrot flies. There are also many health benefits from rosemary: it is known to improve digestion and relieve constipation, it has pain-relieving and anti-cancer properties, and it may also improve blood circulation and decrease inflammation.

## *Thyme*

**Thyme** is an easy plant to grow and great for beginners who are just starting out. This herb prefers soil that is well draining and full of organic material. It does really well in soils that have a pH between 6.5 and 7.0. The ideal temperature should be around 60°F to 70°F. This plant can be kept near your rosemary since it also enjoys full sun. Unlike rosemary, thyme has to be regularly watered, but only when the soil has dried. This practice helps to improve the absorption of nutrients.

Like rosemary, thyme can be grown from either seeds or cuttings. Planting as a seed is pretty straightforward. You can plant them in smaller containers and as soon as they begin to sprout, you can transplant the young seedlings into the garden bed or larger container. Likewise, the cutting can be planted into a soil mix that has already been watered, and then kept in a warm and shaded spot. Once the cuttings begin to take root, you can then pull it out into the sun.

Thyme tastes wonderful, but there are also other lesser-known benefits. Thyme is a spice that has a fairly high amount of tryptophan, an amino acid that serves as the building block for serotonin, which is the body's 'happy hormone'. Boosted levels of serotonin can help anxiety and depression. Thyme may also be beneficial in relieving pain and has anti-inflammatory properties.

## *Basil*

**Basil** is one of the most popular aromatic herbs that you can plant in your greenhouse. It is widely liked for its rich flavor in both sweet and savory dishes. It also provides a good source of vitamin A, vitamin K, calcium, iron, and manganese. Unfortunately, it can sometimes be difficult to grow. Although it's easier than many vegetables and fruits, it requires some maintenance while still in the development process.

Basil needs a rich soil that has a good degree of aeration. The soil should be kept moist and drained. When basil is in environments that have less light, be careful of how much you water it, because it can easily become waterlogged. **Basil can tolerate dry conditions but it cannot tolerate being overwatered**. You can usually tell if the plant has been overwatered when the lowermost leaves have begun to turn yellow. This is usually a good sign that the roots are too wet. Give the soil time to dry out between watering. In fact, this is a great candidate for irrigation systems that allow for scheduled or timed watering.

Basil likes the heat and needs to dwell in a climate of 50°F or more to do well. Basil is also an herb that requires regular pruning to promote further basil leaf growth and to decrease the chance of untimely bolting.

## *Parsley*

Greenhouse **parsley** is simple and easy. While it makes an excellent garnish and seasoning, it is also rich in vitamins such as vitamin C and vitamin K, as well as antioxidants such as flavonoids and carotenoids. Parsley can be planted in almost any container or space. The soil should be moist and rich – usually supplemented by compost. Soil should be maintained at a pH of around 6.0 to 7.0. It should be well-draining and mulched to keep the plant moist and cool.

The optimal temperatures for parsley are between 60°F and 75°F. Parsley also benefits from full sunlight with low shade during hot days. Although parsley is able to produce seedlings in cold conditions, it prefers warmer temperatures.

It's important to note that parsley often has **slow seed growth**. This can be remedied by soaking the seeds before planting. As the seeds sprout and begin to grow, parsley will need to be thinned out as it begins to rise. Parsley should often be individually watered and monitored since seeds can germinate at various times.

## Starting From Seeds

Starting from seeds is a common way for backyard gardeners to save money. Seedlings can be expensive - especially if you're trying to get a whole lot of them. In contrast, seeds are relatively inexpensive. They can run from anywhere between

$1-2 a packet (sometimes even less). Starting seeds in a greenhouse means that you can create a stable and controlled atmosphere for your future plants. You can actually begin planting seeds in greenhouses at any point throughout the year because of this controlled environment!

Usually, people begin seeds within individual trays in greenhouses. Different seeds have different needs. Some seeds need to be soaked before being planted. Others may need a cold environment and then others may need a warm and cold environment followed by a season of dryness.

When deciding on how to plant, consider both open and plug trays. **Plug trays** allow you to separate seedlings in one giant tray, which can help reduce disease and make transplanting a lot easier. **Open trays**, in contrast, are large, undivided trays that you can fill with soil and plant seeds - like a small garden bed. Usually, they're planted in spaced rows for ease of access and care.

However you choose to plant your seeds, remember that they are being prepared for transplantation into the larger garden bed or containers of the greenhouse. Generally, once seeds begin sprouting a few leaves they are ready to transplant into pots or cells. Make sure that these are **true leaves,** meaning the leaves that the plant naturally produces as an adult. Most plants have the initial leaves that show that they are budding and developing. However, these leaves can be misleading, and are not the true leaves of the plant.

Seedlings don't take much to get started. You can use a normal soil mix or make your own. For seeds that you transplant, make sure that you either sterilize the potting mix that you've used for seeding for reuse, or use a brand new potting mix in order to block any potential pathogens that may be lingering behind.

# Maximizing Germination

**Germination** is the process where a seed begins to produce a sprout and form a seedling. Obviously, this is a pretty important process for any prospective backyard gardener. Most seeds are dormant until they receive enough moisture to stimulate growth. As has been mentioned, sometimes you can trick the seed into growing faster by pre-soaking them in water before you put them in the soil. You're trying to signal the plant that it's time to grow without adding too much moisture, because then your seeds may actually begin to rot.

Moisture is not the only thing that helps to stimulate growth: temperature is incredibly important! If temperatures are too hot or cold, germination will be delayed. Even more frustrating, some seedlings may be warmer or colder than others and so some may start to produce faster or slower than others. This can complicate things and cause inconsistencies. Greenhouses tend to be great locations for germination because you can control the temperature of the greenhouse and also insert the entire tray of seedlings or potential seedlings into the greenhouse, and you can ensure they all have the same exact temperature and climate.

Now, your seeds. If you are starting with seeds indoors or if you have seeds that require different temperatures, it's often best to allow the seeds that require colder temperatures to be outside. Then you can seal the seeds that require warmer temperatures into a bag, where they can collect moisture and heat in one place. Alternatively, you can get a small cold or hot box (outlined in **chapter 2**) to help germinate your dormant seeds.

One of the biggest ways to maximize germination is to know your seeds well from the get-go. Some plants, like lavender, will take a long time to germinate in general. Even at its fastest, lavender can take a while to start to seed and sprout. If you have seeds that are supposed to be sprouting soon but you haven't seen any change from them, though, you may want to inspect where you got your seeds from. Sometimes it's possible for seeds to just be duds! Lastly, resist the urge to constantly poke, prod, and move the soil around to see if your seed is sprouting. This can be traumatizing and damaging to the plant and may delay germination even further. Often, the best course of action is to leave your seed in place and practice patience. There's nothing like that sense of anticipation as you wait to see your plants appear!

Chapter 4:

# Greenhouse Maintenance

Your greenhouse is just that. A house for all your green babies! This means you will have to take time to keep this structure clean and maintain it, just like your home. You want to make sure that, similar to how you may do home inspections and seasonal checks, you do the same for your greenhouse.

If you treat your greenhouse well, and are intentional about maintenance, your greenhouse can last you for many years. If you want optimal crops, you need to use an optimal environment. Letting your greenhouse fall into decay or disrepair will only compromise the integrity of your plants. Cracked windows or floors covered in rotting material can lead to disease and a climate that is very difficult to manage.

It can be challenging to keep track of all the daily tasks greenhouse owners must complete on a regular basis. You may find it helpful to keep in mind these **7 simple steps for proper greenhouse maintenance**:

1) Watch your water.
2) Take care of your temperature.
3) Lay out your lighting.
4) Support your soil.
5) Clean your clutter.
6) Review your repairs.
7) Plan for your plants.

Remembering these seven steps will help you avoid missing anything as you try to optimize your greenhouse's potential.

Let's explore how these elements play a role in maintaining a thriving greenhouse environment.

# Creating The Right Environment

The whole purpose of a greenhouse is to create an environment where your plants can thrive. If you have tropical plants, you want to create an environment that is humid and warm. If you have hardy plants that enjoy the cold, then you want to create an environment that is cooler and where shade is plentiful. Here are a few things to consider when creating the right environment.

## *Water*

The way that you manage your water is crucial for a successful greenhouse. You may think that the water you're using is fine, but there could be factors that you are unaware of.

For example, did you know that deep well water is less likely to carry disease, but has a higher pH level and greater mineral content? These small factors can change the consistency of your soil and alter the pH so that your plants produce differently or at different times than you may have originally planned.

Normal water delivered from the city is supposed to be potable for humans; however, as it's distributed through pipes and other vectors, it can become contaminated with various chemicals. Testing your water for quality can help you know how to treat the water or how to better care for your plants. For example, if you know that the water you use has higher pH, you can temper that by adding aluminum sulfate to the soil, which will lower the pH.

In addition to the kind of water you use, how you water your plants is also important for greenhouse maintenance. To maintain healthy plants, you need to water them regularly. Many greenhouses use an **irrigation system** where water is brought in through a hose or drip system. How you set up your irrigation system is entirely up to you. You can even bring water by hand into the greenhouse; however, for larger greenhouses, that's not always practical.

Carrying water can get tiring and take up incredible amounts of time. Often, people will use **capillary mats** to save time and energy. These go underneath your containers or garden beds and release water slowly so that the plant roots can take up water over time. This helps prevent overwatering as well as minimizes evaporation so that the plant is getting the optimal amount of water necessary.

It's best to group your crops by those that have similar watering needs. This makes it easier to water them all at once. You also avoid mixing plants that love more water with plants that need less. Careful watering and timing is important, but when you finish, you may want to water all your containers with just a little bit more water than is necessary. You can collect any runoff or spillage with a collection mat and, unless it's contaminated, send it to be recycled.

Setting up a water system can take time and research. It might also be a little bit frustrating at first, but the benefits of creating a system and putting it in place to deal with your water needs far outweighs the challenges that you may encounter while doing so.

## *Temperature & Humidity*

Maintaining temperature and humidity in your greenhouse is very important. Every plant is different, and usually the ideal greenhouse temperature is between 65°F to 80°F, depending on what you're growing. Temperature has to be maintained at this level because this is an artificial climate that you are creating for your crops. Fortunately, there are many different ways to control the temperature and humidity in your greenhouse.

One of the main and most important ways to manage greenhouse temperature is through the use of sunshine. A greenhouse is created to collect and track heat from the sun. That's how you get the heat in! But, as we've mentioned, plants can be adversely affected by too much heat. In order to manage and release some of that heat, you have to use ventilation. Maybe you want to bring in an actual air circulation unit or just open windows in the greenhouse; you learned a little about ventilation in **Chapter 2**, and you can go back to that chapter any time.

Your humidity is equally important and can be affected by temperature. In general, warmer air tends to hold onto more water. You'll want to keep your humidity level around 80% and manage it through the use of air circulation, as well as drawing dry air into the greenhouse through exhausts or pumps. You can also manage humidity by decreasing the amount of water being sprayed from irrigation systems, or that is present in the garden beds and/or greenhouse floor.

So how do you know your temperature and humidity levels? Well, there are several different tools that make it easy to monitor and maintain your greenhouse temperature and humidity levels. One of the best options is a greenhouse temperature control system. This helps you monitor the current temperature and notes when the temperature falls or rises outside of the optimal range. You can even have an alarm that's attached to it so that it will sound when the temperature is outside of optimal range, or if there has been a power outage of some kind. If you're really willing to spend money, you can even have these sensors automated to open windows and turn on circulation when the temperature has fluctuated outside of the required range, similar to how central heat in a residential home works.

## *Light*

Managing light means using and optimizing light in such a way that it benefits crops the most. Your crops need light to grow, whether that comes from the sun or from an artificial grow light. But understanding light requires more than just plugging in a lightbulb and pointing it at the nearest plant! There are different kinds of light, and each of these has a different effect on plant growth.

Researchers have described light in terms of colors. **Red and blue lights seem to have the greatest effect on plant growth**. Green light does not have much effect on plants in general. Blue light will encourage leaf growth, while red and blue light combined encourage a plant to flower..

The colors present in light are not the only factors that impact your plant. Your crops will also be impacted by how intense the light is and how long they are exposed to it. There are many crops that require a certain ratio of light and dark hours in order to produce fruit. Some crops require indirect sunlight, while others require full sun and light intensity. Being able to manipulate both the intensity and duration of your lights will help you optimize the growth of your crops.

Optimal light conditions are maintained in greenhouses using a variety of different lamps and bulbs. Some of these include incandescent lamps, fluorescent lamps, high-pressure sodium lamps, high-intensity discharge lamps, and complex light emitting diodes. Each of these produce a light of different composition and intensity.

Do research into the kind of a light you think your plants need, as well as how each lamp influences their development. The information you collect can clue you in on what kind of lights to buy and when to use them. When used optimally, artificial lighting is a powerful tool to help create the ideal climate in your greenhouse.

## *Soil*

Do you know what's in your soil? Soil culture or composition helps determine what your crops will be using to grow. **Ideal soil should be well-drained and fertile.** It should also be high in organic matter; in many cases, this means that the soil will be amended with **compost**. Usually, compost is applied before growing vegetables or fruits and it should be well-made so that there are no diseases or pests present before application.

It is possible to create your own compost and maintain it. The process to do so involves using kitchen scraps, discarded leaves, and various other organic materials, gathering them together in an outdoor space, and then covering them in a tarp or holding container for an extended period of time. This allows them to get hot from direct contact with the sun, which speeds up the rate of decomposition. This process can be time-consuming and requires attentiveness. Creating your own compost is cost-effective and a useful way to recycle organic materials, but there are many garden stores that offer compost for sale that you can pick up and apply directly to your soil.

In addition to that organic material, your soil will also need to be checked for a quality pH level. Most fruits and vegetables like a pH level of 6.0 or 7.0, erring on the acidic side. You can buy a soil testing kit at many garden stores. These usually come with a pH meter that you can use to determine the current pH of your soil. If it turns out that your soil is too acidic, you can add components like lime to increase the alkalinity (push the pH more to the basic end of the scale). On the other hand, if it's too alkaline, usually adding organic matter will help increase the acidity. If you require a more dramatic acidity change, you can use elemental sulfur to help lower the pH further.

Many plants benefit from mulching practices. Once your soil is down and your plants are in the ground, water will evaporate and be lost. Heat will also naturally escape your soil bed. **Mulch** can help offset the loss of heat and water while also introducing more nutrients into the ground. This layer is usually applied to the surface of the soil and it can be either made or bought from any local gardening store.

## Cleaning and Upkeep

Of course, like any other space, **a greenhouse requires regular cleaning and upkeep to maintain optimal conditions**. Making this a regular part of your everyday process can help make it feel less like a chore and more like a part of the practice.

You need to clean your greenhouse to remove habitats where diseases and pests will thrive. Routine cleaning helps to remove any insects or pests that may try to hide in the cracks and crevices, as well as pathogens that dwell in plant cutoffs and stagnant water. Cleaning should also include disinfecting and proper safety procedures.

When you are ready to clean your greenhouse, pick a day when you are able to remove your pots, plants, and tools from the space. Make sure that you do not carry any materials or containers directly over live soil beds or currently installed plants as you move your materials around; making sure no water drips from one pot to another can help prevent cross-contamination. Make sure that you are aware of any suspicious pests or plants that may need to be quarantined, isolated, or tossed out altogether. Commit to regular inspections of your plants and tools to ensure that everything looks to be in order.

You may want to use a shop vac on any dirty floors and surfaces before cleaning and sanitizing them. You don't want any soil residue or other substances to interfere with the cleaning solutions that you use. High-pressure power washing is also useful for scrubbing and rinsing with soap and water.

Good practice usually involves starting at the top and making your way down. This keeps the places you've cleaned from getting re-contaminated. Begin by removing any buildup on your windows and roof area, moving carefully downward. The floor should be the last thing you clean in your greenhouse because it collects the water and debris you wash off everything above. Once you are done with all the higher surfaces, you can wash the floor and remove all the dirt and debris at once.

This is also an opportunity to throw away any containers or old soil that has been used before. If the containers are reusable, wash them and thoroughly disinfect them with a bleach solution of ¾ cup of bleach to 1 gallon of water. **Be very careful with bleach.** This can be extremely toxic to plants and any other helpful organisms that may be nearby. If you are unable to move plants away from your cleaning area, you can also use cleaning vinegar. While not as powerful as bleach, vinegar is a safer alternative if it somehow gets into your pots. Throw out any old soil and replace it with clean soil that has not been exposed to the elements or contaminated plant life.

Make sure to utilize clean water sources and check any nozzles and sitting water for algae or fungi. Disinfect the irrigation systems before replacing them or changing out the plants that they service. Make sure to manage algae by regularly disinfecting and caring for your space.

Finally, even after you've done all the cleaning in your greenhouse, you need to make sure that you yourself are clean. Proper hygiene, regular monitoring, and awareness can help you keep from tracking pests as well as disease into your greenhouse. It's often helpful to have a place nearby where you can wash your hands or change out any gloves.

## *Common Repairs*

Nobody likes to hear this, but eventually, everything breaks down. That's why proper maintenance can help prevent expensive repairs in the future. Even with the most effective preventative practices, though, you will eventually need to make some repairs. That's just part of the maintenance process! Here are a few common repairs that you can expect when having a greenhouse.

One of the most obvious repairs that you'll probably have to make at some point involves the **glazing or window**. Even the toughest windows can be prone to accidents. As durable as they are, you should be ready to note any cracks or chips that you might find. These can compromise the integrity of the window and make it more susceptible to breaking. Identifying and taking care of these problems early can help avoid a potentially painful and expensive disaster.

Keep an eye on your doors and seals as well as ventilation. These are exposed to the elements and therefore can get weathered rather quickly. Using them regularly also causes natural wear and tear. If you notice them making strange sounds, sticking, or not working as well as they used to, take note. If you notice any sealant that is starting to peel away or decay, take note. Replace or repair these issues while they are small.

**Hoses and irrigation systems are susceptible to cracks over time** and can often start to leak water out of these cracks. They can also be susceptible to dirt or debris buildup which can cause deposits that make it hard to install or remove nozzles, screws, and other attachments.

If you have fans, heaters, or any other automated equipment, make sure that you lubricate the moving parts regularly and that you run them periodically to make sure that they are in good working order. Keep an eye and an ear out for any shaking or unnatural sounds, as well as any sounds that would indicate dirt or debris getting caught inside the system.

## *Managing Mold*

Managing mold is such a challenging ordeal that it deserves a section all to itself. At some point you're probably going to run into a mold problem during your greenhouse gardening career. With the combination of warm temperatures and a moist environment, you are creating the ideal habitat for mold to grow. While regular cleaning and maintenance can help offset the appearance of mold, you will also need to know what to do once you do find it.

Mold and mildew are both **fungi**. Often these are spread by the spores that they produce. When you have warm temperatures, standing water, and poor air circulation, mold is more likely to grow and spread. While there are many different kinds of mold, and most are not considered harmful, there are many that can damage plants and humans as well.

To help prevent mold and mildew, you can keep your humidity below 85% and try to avoid overwatering your plants. You can also increase ventilation and promote air circulation by opening windows or turning on a fan to keep the air moving. Throw out any stagnant or standing water and maintain an overall environment of cleanliness.

If you do get mold, there are ways that you can handle it. The first is to identify the location and, ideally, the type of mold that you have. **The most common molds that you might find in a greenhouse, either on plants or the actual walls of your greenhouse, is mildew, black sooty mold, or gray mold**. No matter what type of mold you have, the solution is pretty much the same. Mold found on flowers or plants needs to be removed immediately to prevent spreading. This is especially the case for black sooty mold, which may require an extra step - tracking down the pests that produce the honeydew that it grows on. **Be careful when moving plants so that you don't allow the spores to spread to the uncontaminated plants.** After you have removed the plants, burning or burying them is probably the best solution to make sure that these molds don't spread further.

For mold that's found on or around your greenhouse, you can clean it off with hydrogen peroxide or a cleaning vinegar solution. Simply spray either on the mold as you see it, wait about 30 minutes to an hour, and then clean it off with water. Make sure to scrub and dry the area afterward to prevent more mold from showing up. You can also use a bleach solution to clean your mold problem. This is considered a more combative solution, but remember, it can damage your plants if they are not distanced substantially from the location.

# Planning Your Space

Greenhouse interior design? Yes, please! There is something fun about creating a brand-new environment to dwell in. Although this environment is primarily for your plants, you will spend a lot of time there. A good greenhouse is a relaxing place where you can go take a load off and participate in the miracle of growing. In order to help facilitate this, it's important to have a practical and low-stress greenhouse layout.

One of the easiest things you can do to arrange your greenhouse is to decide what **zones** you're going to have. These are areas dedicated to the basic practices of maintaining a greenhouse. Perhaps that means you outline an area dedicated to cutting and potting. Another area may be dedicated to storage and contain various shelves and cabinetry.

Along those lines, it's important to have a section that is completely dedicated to keeping your tools and supplies safe. You need to keep them out of the walk path and away from any liquids or debris that could rust or decay them in any way. This area should include space for soil, compost, fertilizer, and any other garden preparation materials. Keep these in a separate location from your tools and gloves and other safety items.

Another good idea when planning your greenhouse is to **have a section dedicated to quarantine or isolation**. There should be a section that is closed off in some way, so you don't spread pests or diseases to any of your other plants. This is especially important if you find yourself adding plants often, bringing them from another location into the ecosystem that is your greenhouse.

When deciding where you're putting your plants, make sure that you put those that require the most sun on the side of the greenhouse where the sun is most prevalent. It's helpful to have these on a high shelf where they can be away from any shade that other plants might provide. Likewise, your hardier and shade-requiring plants should be in a location of the greenhouse where the sun does not reach all the time.

You also may want to consider a dedicated section for seedlings and other nursery-level plants. In many cases, these may require warmer or more humid environments. Since heat rises, it's good to keep them well off the ground, but keeping them separate also allows for the space that many of the trays and carts you'll use will need.

Most of all, make sure that your space has plenty of room for your crops. It can be very easy to try to cram a lot of plants in a small space! But airflow between plants can help prevent disease as well as pests. You also don't want your plants to be crowded out by the shade from surrounding plants or touching plants of a different section.

If you find yourself uncertain about how to arrange your plants, or if you just like to switch things up every now and then, consider using containers that are lighter so that they are easy to move. You can also put benches on wheels so that you can move them around as necessary to create different formations and arrangements.

## Your Daily Checklist

In order to keep your greenhouse operating at very high standards, you need to make sure that every day you are adjusting and making small changes as necessary. Many backyard greenhouse owners have found that coming up with a checklist is the easiest way to remember these daily maintenance items.

The following sample checklist can help you stay on top of the daily duties involved with maintaining a successful greenhouse. It doesn't include any of the deep cleaning or soil exchange that would normally happen on a seasonal or semi-annual basis; this is just a list of some basics you should be doing every time you spend time in your greenhouse.

## *Daily Greenhouse Maintenance Checklist*

**Outside**

- Do a greenhouse "walk around."
    - Check for cracked or damaged windows.
    - Check for and close any gaps where pests or debris can get in.
    - *Optional:* Check glazing to make sure clips are securely in place.
- Note any nearby pest nests or colonies.

**Inside**

- Clean and disinfect surfaces (shelves, benches, etc.).
- Inspect surfaces or walls for algae or mold.
- Inspect windows and doors for any air leaks or worn caulking.
- Inspect plants - isolate any diseased or infected produce.
- Test any automated systems.
- Monitor tools for signs of rust or decay.
- Wash floors of any soil or plant debris.

# Chapter 5:

# Good Pest - Bad Pest

Your crops aren't the only thing that will be trying to grow and thrive in your greenhouse. Unfortunately, the same temperate climate created by the greenhouse that extends the growing season of your garden also creates an optimal environment for various insects, which find greenhouses to be a comfortable location to live and reproduce. However, not every critter with multiple legs should be banned! In fact, there are several that can be beneficial. Knowing how to identify and understand these pests can tell you if the bug-eyed creature you see is a friend or foe.

These pests plague both commercial and casual growers alike. This chapter will explore some of the common pests as well as ways you can control and reduce their damage - without pesticides.

## Bad Pests

### *Aphids*

**Aphids** are one of the most common greenhouse pests. One of the reasons they're so well-known is because of their **high reproductive rate**. They also tend to be resistant to various insecticides and can get out of control very quickly. One reason they reproduce so quickly is that most aphids are female, who

73

then give birth to live young that are already carrying nymphs – baby aphids. They completely skipped the egg stage and are already at the stage of eating plant sap.

Aphids are very small pear-shaped insects with long legs and antennae. They feed by drinking the sap of your plants. While they usually like the more-visible, growing parts of the plant, they are also known to be found underneath the plants, on the roots, and almost anywhere else. As they suck up nutrients, they simultaneously excrete a sugary substance called **honeydew** on the plant. Fungi can grow on that honeydew which can stunt photosynthesis.

One of the best things you can do to prevent aphids is to regularly scout your plants for signs. **You'll be looking for little white or greenish dots**. You may also be able to find signs of honeydew - and potentially the mold that grows on it. Also, if you put some sticky paper out, you may be able to catch flying aphids. These forms only begin to appear when an aphid colony is growing out of control and is using up all the resources. Their purpose is to migrate to other locations for food. Unfortunately, sticky paper will only catch your flying aphids, not the non-winged ones.

One of the main ways that you can help control the aphid population in your greenhouse is to introduce predatory and parasitic enemies. Creatures like the green lacewing or the parasitic wasp can feed on the aphids and decrease their population. These wasps tend to lay their eggs inside the larva of whiteflies and when those eggs hatch, they eat them from the inside out. Not the prettiest picture to imagine, but certainly a better outcome for your garden.

This is the most popular non-chemical solution. You may also want to plant things like marigold and catnip, which are known for having a scent that keeps aphids away. Other fragrant herbs like dill, cilantro, chives, and oregano are also known for secreting oils and scents to deter aphids.

## *Thrips*

**Thrips** are some of the most annoying pests that you can find in your greenhouse! Due to their small size, they can be challenging to find before they've already started to wreak havoc on your plants. Sometimes this damage can show on foliage as white or gray patches on top of leaves. Like the aphid, they feed by inserting their mouthparts into the plants and sucking out the sap. This can also be a problem because thrips will spread viruses from one plant to another.

Like aphids, most thrips are females. They do lay eggs that grow into larvae and eventually into adults. It's important to monitor for these thrips every 10 to 14 days. You'll be looking for areas that are not exposed, like a garden bed or a sheltered area. You'll also want to look for the little black excrement dots that they tend to leave behind. Keep an eye out for plants that have white patches or bleached tissue. Lastly, thrips usually gather in colonies. If you find one, there's bound to be more, so look for them in larger amounts.

The best way to deal with thrips is to not deal with them at all. Try to keep them out of your greenhouse as much as possible. Frequently check to be aware of where and how many threats are gathering. If you do find plants that are infested, make sure to isolate them to avoid the spreading of the pests. Natural enemies like parasitic wasps and other egg parasites can help to deal with young and larval thrips. However, many predators are often deterred by thrips due to the **black fecal excrement** that they produce.

## *Slugs/snails*

While both **snails** and **slugs** can be damaging to your plants, slugs are definitely the worst of the two. Most of these techniques for management used in this section will apply to both, though. Both slugs and snails like to feed on the tissue of plants. Slugs use their incredible rows of teeth to chew through plant tissue and devour the nutrients inside the plant that your crops need to survive. Slugs, like many of the dreaded pests we've been going through, have both sexes and can present as male or female depending on what is needed for reproduction at the time. This allows them to reproduce efficiently. Their eggs are not always noticeable and will require intention on your part to find them.

One of the best ways of managing slugs is to keep a tidy area. That means cleaning your garden tools – you don't want to add to the problem by bringing pests into your own greenhouse – and making sure that there is no loose brush, damp wood, or other debris laying around that they could hide under. These creatures usually feed at night after hiding throughout the day underneath debris.

Another way to manage slugs is to build a barrier between your plants and wherever you presume the slugs might be. Both snails and slugs have very soft bodies and don't travel well over rough surfaces. With that logic, some have found success when they lay down gravel or other rough and dry surfaces around their garden as they tend to avoid those uncomfortable surfaces. You can also lay out beer traps. This may sound like an odd solution to the problem, but the smell of beer attracts these pests and they drown when entering the beer can. Unfortunately, you may have to spend a lot of time emptying the cans, but it does solve the problem and utilizes what may be, for some, an item they already have in their home.

Nematodes have been discovered to be powerful and effective predators against slugs and snails. Usually, they are watered around the soil and onto the plants. They kill off their prey by entering their bodies and producing a bacteria that infects them. Eventually, this causes their prey to die.

## *Whiteflies*

Like aphids, **whiteflies** feed on plant sap. They tend to look like small white triangles. Also, like aphids, they produce honeydew, which again can attract black sooty mold. These creatures are very tiny but reproduce quickly and can seriously destroy and wreak havoc on your greenhouse. Their eggs are usually laid on the underside of leaves and the eggs quickly hatch into nymphs, who stay at the same location feeding until they can grow wings as adults. This entire process can take as little as three weeks.

It's important to notice the presence of whiteflies as soon as they appear. You might get hints about their presence when you start seeing plants that are turning yellow and wilting. You might see small white dots all over a part of the plant. You might also notice the sticky honeydew, especially if it is starting to attract mold. You may also want to keep any new plants isolated for one to two weeks to see if anything appears. Generally, whiteflies can't survive in cold environments, so you're more apt to see them in warm, dry seasons. This means that greenhouse gardeners living in southern climates should pay particular attention. As the seasons change, you should be especially attentive to the state of your crops and monitor for any suspicious, uninvited guests.

There are several different ways that you can manage these pests. You can use yellow sticky cards to catch them, which can be purchased from any garden supply store. Noticing multiple whiteflies on your sticky card per day can give you a hint that there may be an infestation. You can also use a hose to knock whiteflies off the plants if there is a large amount of them present at one time. In addition, you can use insecticidal soap, many of which are organic and will not infect your plant with pesticides. If you're particularly concerned about buying store brands, you can even make your own – there are many different tutorials and recipes online, and you're sure to find one that will work for you. Lastly, parasitic wasps are effective predators that can clear out these pests.

## Good Pests

As you may have noticed, not all the creepy crawlies you find in your greenhouse may be enemies. Some are great at taking down the creatures that can cause the greatest damage to your crops. Some are needed by your crops to be more successful. Let's take a look at a few examples of friends you may (or rather, should!) have in your greenhouse.

### *Bumblebee*

There are usually two schools of people: those who run in terror at the first sight of a bee, and the people who calmly notice their striped, fuzzy friends and are grateful they stopped by. If you're the former, take note that the **bumblebee** is one bee that you will want to warmly welcome in your greenhouse. In fact, many people intentionally introduce bumblebees into their greenhouses in order to help their plants. Our plants need pollen to produce fruit and bees help with that process!

**There is arguably no better pollinator than a bumblebee.** Because of their size, they can carry a lot more pollen from plant to plant as they move and go about their daily duties. Do you know the phrase "busy bee?" Well, it's well-deserved! Bees are incredible workers and don't stop, ever. Bumblebees are also a great option because they're less aggressive than other bees and thus, safer. Bumblebees tend to be very effective in small environments like greenhouses. Honeybees struggle because they use the sun to determine their location and they often don't understand that they can't fly through glass panels. They also tend to place their nests in higher locations.

Bumblebees are more apt to find alternative locations to create their homes. Many are ground-dwelling creatures and may take advantage of abandoned nests, leaf litter, and even loose soil. Bees like this tend to like the warm, humid environment that the greenhouse provides and would be very happy to live and work with you.

To attract these bees, as well as others that may provide help for your greenhouse, you need to make sure that they have access to the inside. You can open your roof, ventilation windows, or leave the door of your greenhouse open. You also want plants that will attract them inside. Plants like lemon balm, lavender, and fennel can be grown inside and outside of your greenhouse to encourage them to follow the road inside. Bees may also benefit from a place where they can reach water, along with crevices, wood, and holes that they can make their home.

## *Praying Mantis*

The **praying mantis** must be mentioned here as a friendly option for pest management. This is one of the most fun insects that you can have in your greenhouse, but also one of the most controversial. Unlike many other bugs that manage and specifically target damaging pests, the praying mantis will strike out indiscriminately at any pest in sight. Yes, this means both good and bad pests are in harm's way when a praying mantis is around! That being said, it's definitely good at its job.

The praying mantis usually starts as an egg and eventually, over the course of several weeks of warm weather, will hatch into small babies that continually molt until they reach their adult form.

While having multiple praying mantises in a greenhouse can be a good thing, because they try to eat any insect that moves, they often aren't great for targeting your preferred pest population. So, if you have a whitefly population that is getting out of control, there is no guarantee that the mantis will focus entirely on the whitefly population. They may focus on the whitefly population as well as the bumblebee population as well as the wasp population as well as...you get the picture. That being said, it's a very good option to consider when you're trying to fill your greenhouse with additional beneficial predators.

## *Lady Beetle (Ladybug)*

**Ladybugs** are another fun insect to include in your greenhouse defense. Ladybugs are very well known for their fashionable attire; however, they also have a voracious appetite as babies, and they are very effective at managing aphid populations. Growers will often buy large quantities of ladybugs and release them into their greenhouse to manage aphid populations.

These insects can usually be ordered from various supply stores. They often come packed with packing straw in a linen bag. Even though you may have purchased a large number of ladybugs, as tempting as it would be, you don't want to race home and haphazardly dump them all into your greenhouse. You want to make sure that you use them effectively. If you're introducing ladybugs to your greenhouse for the first time, make sure that you are using a variety that is native to your area so that they do not bring any foreign disease. You should also know what young ladybugs look like. They can look a bit scary – kind of like spiky, six-legged caterpillars. Make sure to be familiar with their young form so that you don't accidentally start getting rid of them.

**When introducing ladybugs to the environment, do so a little bit at a time** and try to keep them centered on the area where you want them to live and eat. Many people will keep ladybugs in smaller areas like seedling carts or small beds. Sometimes they may even cover these areas with a cloth to train them to stay in that location.

One of the great things about ladybugs is that they become dormant when you put them in cold temperatures, so any ladybugs you choose not to use can be stored safely in the fridge. Just be sure to warn any insect-averse family members or you'll have a whole new problem on your hands

## *Lacewing*

**Green lacewings** are known as the **aphid lion** for a reason. No other predator consumes nearly as many aphids in the same amount of time as a lacewing. These predators will also happily eat creatures with a soft body, including mealy bugs, caterpillar eggs, thrips, and whiteflies.

Lacewing larvae are the main attackers in this process. Lacewing will lay eggs that eventually hatch into larvae, and these larvae will climb the stalk of the plant that they were laid on and inject venom into their prey to drain out its body fluids. After a few weeks of eating, larvae will spin cocoons and emerge in several days as adults, fully prepared to lay eggs.

It's best to release lacewings either in the early morning or in the later afternoon when it is a bit cooler out. It's also best to release them as soon as you bring them home, but if you are unable to do so, you can refrigerate them for a short time –

similar to ladybugs – and they should be fine. You can usually order lacewing eggs, and they are often shipped with moth eggs so that when they hatch, they can use the moth eggs as food. Don't be alarmed if you see double the amount of eggs you expected!

Chapter 6:

# Dealing With Disease

For lack of a better word, diseases are simply annoying. It can be frustrating to see that your plant babies are sick and feel powerless to help them. They can wreak havoc on our bodies and they can wreak havoc on our crops, too! But they are a reality, and so we have to figure out how to deal with them. This chapter will look at some of the most common diseases you may find in your greenhouse, as well as basic practices you can use to prevent and treat them.

## Common Greenhouse Diseases

Just like with humans, there are many different illnesses that can afflict your plants. In **chapter 4** we talked about planning for a section of the greenhouse to be dedicated to quarantine and isolation; this is where that dedicated area comes into play. As we talk about common greenhouse diseases, make note of what you learn. When you have plants that seem to meet any of the following symptoms or characteristics, immediately remove them and place them in the isolation area for further inspection. Don't risk contaminating the healthy plants by keeping the sick ones close by!

## *Bacterial Wilt*

Researchers and agriculturalists have done a lot of work studying bacterial wilt. As a backyard greenhouse beginner, the important thing is that this is a major disease and can come in two forms. The first form is **Race 1**, which is native to the United States and, while endemic and damaging, is more manageable. The other form, **Race 3**, is not native to the United States and is federally quarantined.

**Bacterial wilt** appears as - you guessed it - wilting on the leaves of the plant. Often this comes with yellowing and leaf decay. Usually, the bacteria infects mainly plants of the same family. **Nightshade vegetables like eggplants and tomatoes are especially at risk.** Wilt can spread rapidly from plant to plant, and transmission can be especially triggered when disease cuttings are left scattered around your greenhouse, so make sure you dispose of them! This disease can also stunt the growth of the plants suddenly and even when fruits are already growing on it.

In some plants, you may see long brown streaks or a sticky, milky white substance on the surface of the cut portions of infected stems. Usually, these are the bacterially infected tissues coming out of the stem. When placed under clear water, sometimes you can see it a lot more clearly.

There are not many ways to treat this disease, so your goal should be to constantly stay aware of any suspicious-looking plants that are wilting or showing any of the signs. Generally, you should keep those plants where they are, wrap them in a plastic garbage bag, and then keep them in a cool area for testing later. If you do find that you have bacterial wilt, you will need to disinfect the greenhouse and consistently monitor all your plants to make sure that the wilt has been exterminated. Any suspicious plant will need to undergo the same treatment.

## *Erwinia*

**Erwinia**, also known as **soft rot**, loves greenhouse environments. This bacterium is well-known for secreting enzymes that can turn your leaves and roots into a mushy mess. It's everywhere as well, meaning that it can be very hard to manage. The bacteria can explode into reproduction and the more there are, the worse the rot.

Erwinia can also get in through any wounds that the plant may have. Thus, **freshly cut plants or plants that have bruises or broken skin are more greatly at risk for infection**. Symptoms of soft rot include damp and soft lesions on leaves, a nasty smell, and sticky or slimy stems.

To beat soft rot, you will need to get rid of any infected plants immediately. Bacteria can spread from them to healthy plants through water, clothes (including your gardening gloves!), and any other transport. You'll also want to inspect your water and make sure that the water is clean and safe. Splashing can often spread soft rot.

Lowering humidity levels in the greenhouse takes away the ideal environment for living and reproducing. Finally, disinfecting the greenhouse with an approved disinfectant could help kill off any lingering trace of the bacterium.

## *Root Rot*

**Root rot** is a common disease that attacks plants, especially in the spring. This disease is primarily caused by a variety of pathogenic fungi. There are many different kinds, and part of dealing with this is being able to identify and diagnose which pathogen you have in your greenhouse. However, many backyard greenhouse owners are unable or unwilling to do so. It is more practical to simply identify the symptoms of potential root rot.

As the name suggests, this disease is primarily found in the **root system of infected plants**. Usually, you can identify potential problems by stunted growth. As you are inspecting the plant, you may notice that the roots are waterlogged and mushy. You should also look for soft and discolored tissue around the stem or brown lesions that are continuously growing.

This can be very hard to treat, especially without the use of fungicide. If you wish to avoid a chemical solution, the best way to handle the problem is to prevent it from happening altogether. One of the key ways to do this is by improving the drainage of your soil. This may mean inspecting the soil composition closely, including the substrate and the size of the particles. This may also mean mixing supplemental materials into the soil like twigs and branches to help create room for water to continue to move.

You might also consider heating your soil to around 180°F or more to kill off any pathogens before they take hold. You may also examine your water treatment to make sure that there is no sediment or infected water. Some people will do ultra-radiant light treatments while others will use filtering. Be careful that you don't over-fertilize! You can compromise a plant's natural defense response by exposing them to too much nitrogen.

The biggest issue that you will likely run into is overwatering. Overwatering provides the ideal climate and habitat for pathogens to grow and thrive.

## *Powdery Mildew*

**Powdery mildew** is both common and usually not lethal to the plant. It can be spread by various fungi. Although this fungus is not destructive, when you're trying to sell your produce, this will reduce the value and appearance.

Powdery mildew is identifiable by the white, soft, downey fungus that grows on the infected parts of the plant. Most commonly, the fungus attacks developing plants but has also been known to dwell within mature crops as well.

Powdery mildew usually appears in low light and high humidity. The ideal conditions for this fungus are high temperatures overnight, and it does not require a lot of water to begin colonizing and destroying plants.

While the downy-like growth of the fungus is the most notable symptom of infection, you may also be able to notice infection based on necrotic lesions or leaves that shrivel and drop prematurely.

Like most of the diseases on this list, prevention is the best form of dealing with this disease. Keeping a greenhouse clean can help prevent interaction or cross-contamination with any infected weeds or other plant clippings. Also, managing the humidity in the greenhouse and keeping it below 93% can help to reduce humidity during the night when it is more likely for the plant to be infected.

## *Impatiens Necrotic Spot Virus (INSV)*

This disease is one of the most common viruses in the plant world. Unfortunately, it is deadly and extremely hard to treat once it's been contracted. As long as it's been infected, the plant is unable to be sold or shared anywhere and it must be destroyed immediately. **INSV** is very contagious and will infect any plant it comes in contact with. There are a lot of different symptoms, including yellow bull's-eye markings, ring spots, lesions, or an inability to produce.

This virus is most commonly transmitted through the western flower thrips. If you remember from **Chapter 5**, thrips are annoying creatures that can be very difficult to manage without the use of pesticides or extensive use of natural enemies like parasitic wasps and other egg parasites. However, the presence of thrips does not mean that your plants are infected. Unless you already have an infected plant, the others can't receive the disease.

Once you've found suspicious plants, place them in quarantine and keep them far away from your regular plants. If they come in contact with them, they could spread the virus. Anytime you bring in new plants, make sure to isolate them to ensure that they do not have the virus before connecting them with the rest of your greenhouse. Again, infected plants must be destroyed. If western flower thrips are not present in your greenhouse, the virus can only be spread from plant to plant via tools or direct contact with the infected produce.

## An Ounce of Prevention

This chapter can be a little frightening if you don't understand what you're looking at. The last chapter was focused on small but noticeable and easy-to-understand insects which feed on the outside of your plants. This chapter, however, has been focused on microscopic and sometimes-invisible enemies to your greenhouse. In many of these cases, the condition cannot be treated and the infected plants must be eliminated as soon as possible.

As we've gone over time and time again, taking care of your greenhouse and maintaining it in a functional and sanitary way can prevent many problems well before they begin.

One easy way to prevent disease is to regularly clean up any debris or clippings that may be left behind. As you prune your plants or bring in new plants, there will inevitably be leaves, flowers, and even produce that fall and collect on floors, shelves, and other surfaces.

Your temptation may be to just leave them there. After all, they are biodegradable, right? Plus, this is a greenhouse – it's going to be a little messy. But the truth is, when you leave these clippings around, they provide the perfect location for fungus and disease to hang out, especially if all the light, temperature, and humidity conditions are perfect. Getting rid of your plant debris and cleaning up any extra clippings can go a long way to denying these diseases the habitat they need to grow and thrive.

Regular sanitation is a proactive practice to prevent disease. During the COVID-19 pandemic we learned how important it is to wipe down surfaces and shared tools. The same goes for inside the greenhouse, where more diseases thrive than you may know. Regularly sanitizing your tools, shelves, and plant areas can help prevent the propagation of disease in your greenhouse. Make sure that you use a cleaner that is strong enough to destroy any microbial pests!

Monitoring the climate is also a good practice. As mentioned before, humidity levels can encourage disease colonization. Make sure that the temperature is high enough for your plants but not in excess, as this could encourage the growth of fungi or bacteria. This also includes maintaining good ventilation and air circulation in your greenhouse. Even if it doesn't feel humid, moisture levels can create a damp enough climate for diseases to thrive. Keep humidity levels as low as you need for the crops that you are growing.

While many spores and bacteria are transmitted through soil and air, water provides another pathway for disease. Make sure that any irrigation arrangements that you have do not leave excessive moisture on plants. Also, be sure that splashing is kept to the absolute minimum. You can avoid splashing altogether by setting up a grounded irrigation system. Any watering that you do should be at the base of the plant, not above or further away. This keeps the water focused on each individual plant and, if a plant is infected, the water will not pick up any of the microbes and transport them as it splashes onto the new plant.

Any new plants that you bring into the greenhouse should be quarantined and isolated for a short period of time (around three days to one week) before you bring them into the greenhouse. It's important to ensure that any new plants are disease-free before they take up residence. Since plant-to-plant contact is the easiest way to transport diseases, reducing the contact helps reduce the likelihood of the disease being contracted by your resident crops.

Chapter 7:

# Harvest Time!

Harvesting is the great reward for all your hard work: now you get the opportunity to collect your bounty! But the work is not done, yet. There is much to consider when preparing to harvest your crops. Enjoy your rewards but keep these points in mind as you do so!

## Timing is Everything

Timing plays a critical role in the entire greenhouse building and development process. You should be performing research on the crops you choose to grow well-before harvest time comes. Knowing when the ideal harvest periods are is critical to making sure that your crops maintain their integrity and that you get them off the stem, vine, or branch at their very best.

Picking them at the best time is not the only factor at play when it comes to getting the best flavor out of your crops. Lots of elements like soil and water can play a role in the taste of your produce; however, timing is still one of the most important factors. Most produce should be picked right before it reaches full maturity, when both texture and taste are at their best.

Understanding the timing of your produce will also ensure that you don't miss the critical harvest moments. For example, broccoli growing in a garden will eventually flower, so you will need to understand the timing of broccoli to harvest it before that happens. Cucumbers are another vegetable that should be harvested while still developing. Cucumbers that are over-ripened can be bitter; however, cucumbers that are harvested young provide the cool refreshing flavor that we know and love.

Timing the harvest of your produce comes down to paying very close attention to your plants. You can time it by weeks, the appearance of the crop, or by feel and touch. You should be aware of how your crop will present in all these ways well-before you reach harvest season.

## Size Your Crop

As we mentioned, size is a big indicator as to whether or not a crop is ready for harvest. However, you can't lean too heavily on that principle! Often, the best time to pull a plant (when it is the most ready and tasty) can come long before the fruit gets to its maximum size. In fact, many plants should never get to their largest size, because they become tough, woody, or pithy, and these don't make for great eating.

When considering size, also consider how easy it is for the crop to be picked and removed. For some plants, they are harvested best when they can be removed from the stem or vine with little effort. Some of them may automatically fall off the vine or stem if left for too long.

Size also impacts storage ability. If you're trying to preserve or keep your crops for later, larger crops may be harder to store and preserve. Some crops continue to ripen after they've been removed from the plant, too. In those cases, sometimes you want to harvest them early so that they ripen at their peak. This means that you shouldn't wait until they are at their maximum size before removing them.

## Stay Attentive

Regularly monitoring your crops during this time is a critical practice. You should take walkthroughs of your garden area every couple of days at the very least. This way, you can note any crops that look ready for harvest. Some crops seem to ripen in a matter of seconds, while others take a much longer time to do so. To make sure that you are there for these key milestones, you will need to be present and regularly visit your crops during the harvest season.

This is also the time when many of your crops can become prey to pests and different types of illnesses. Many pests will be able to sense the fruit ripening and you may end up racing these buggers to your precious harvest! You also don't want to let heavy fruits and vegetables begin to sag or rot in place, as this can be a breeding ground for disease. Trimming and pruning fruits and vegetables that aren't producing or are ready to be picked is part of maintaining a healthy greenhouse.

## Some Basic Techniques

### *Pinching vs. Pruning*

When plants begin to grow tall, sometimes you may want to force them to grow more of their leaves or stems. **Pinching** is a technique where you put your thumb and forefinger on the main stem and squeeze while carefully pulling in order to remove the main stem and force the plant to grow new stems. This encourages your plants to grow fuller with more individual stems, instead of maintaining a few single, long, spidery stems, and this can help your plant have more options for produce. You'll want to do this from immediately above the leaf nodes, which are usually those tiny buds or bumps at the base of the stem where new growth begins. Alternatively, you can use garden shears to help you pinch the end before removing the stem. Make sure you do this as close to the leaf nodes as possible, or your plant might not get the signal to start new growth!

**Pruning**, on the other hand, refers to shaping the plants overall. Pinching is a form of pruning because pruning can be done with your fingers, pruners, cutters, or any of the shears that we talked about in **chapter 1**. Pruning, however, has to do with clipping the plant to achieve your desired fullness. Pinching is about stimulating growth and encouraging production. Pruning is great for leaves and plants that are getting bushy and are beginning to block nutrients and sunlight from smaller, more immature leaves and produce.

When harvesting produce, it's good to know which of these methods you'll need to employ. Pinching is great for smaller plants like herbs where you can easily move and quickly try to harvest your small plants. Pruning, however, is needed for bigger plants and fruits. This can include zucchini, watermelon, and any other vined produce.

## *Minimizing Damage*

Even if you get your produce all-the-way grown and ready for harvest, you aren't out of the woods yet! The harvesting process can be a very violent and traumatic experience for your vegetables and fruits. In fact, this is where much of the damage happens. Proper timing is going to be very important as you try to figure out when and how to harvest your vegetables. The first step to minimizing damage is to know what time of the day is best to work through your harvest. For example, any plants that begin to lose quality throughout the day with increasing high temperatures should probably be picked first thing in the morning before the temperatures get too hot. Knowing your plants, and understanding how they produce their sugars and nutrients, as well as the time of day they like most, will be helpful to determine the best time for harvest.

Another factor that helps reduce the damage to fresh produce is handling. This is where vegetables and fruits end up getting broken skin and cuts and bruises. No matter how you choose to collect your produce, whether in boxes, bags, or any other container, you need to make sure that the container is prepared for their arrival. That means that you should remove any rough edges or places where the produce can be hurt (or you, for that matter)!

You may also want to consider using padding to cushion any produce you place or carry in those containers. A lot of damage can happen en route when you are transporting plants from point A to point B. Along those lines, be careful when you are carrying, pushing, or pulling any produce. These practices can easily end with you stepping on stems or tripping over plants and will end with injury to yourself or the poor produce. Try to avoid pulling or yanking motions. Instead, carefully and consistently apply pressure as you pull any fruits or vegetables that seem to be a bit harder to remove. Yanking could result in tearing off part of the produce or injury to oneself.

## *Washing Practices*

For many people, the idea of being able to pick a fruit or vegetable straight off the vine and pop it into their mouth is an attractive one and it's also part of the reason that they started backyard gardening in the first place. While this may be possible every now and then, when you're doing your actual harvesting from your greenhouse, you want to consider how you're going to take care of the fruits and vegetables that you collect.

Generally, if you're picking a large harvest, you can set up a couple of buckets and fill them with drinking water. For many vegetables and fruits, you will not need to wash them immediately. When you wash them too soon, you risk prematurely removing any protective film that they may have. Usually, the purpose of the film is to protect the fruit or vegetable from insects and bacteria. You can see this very plainly on blueberries, apples, and grapes. However, if you know that you are going to sell them soon or consume them soon, you can go ahead and wash them.

For plants like root vegetables, and leafy vegetables like cabbage and lettuce, washing them immediately is good practice. You can dunk them in the first bucket and, if they are not too dirty, you can go ahead and store them. However, if they are fairly dirty, dunking them in the first bucket will remove the initial dirt collected, and then you can follow up with a second dunk in another bucket to finish washing off the dirt and dust.

After you are done harvesting and preparing your produce, it's now time to think about how you are going to store them. In this day and age there are many different ways for you to provide long-term and short-term storage for even the most finicky crop. We'll explore some of those options in the next chapter.

# Chapter 8:

# Storage and Care

If you've made it to the point in the harvest season where you're starting to look back and read this chapter, it likely means that your harvest was successful this year, and that is worth celebrating! However, it can also be daunting to think about what to do with all of that bountiful harvest. This chapter is designed to be a short guide for the beginner on the preservation and storage of the fruits of your labor - no pun intended! We will be going over some of the tried-and-true methods of food preservation that have been used for centuries, many of which are foolproof and beginner-friendly.

## Long Term Preservation

### *Dry Storage*

The most old-fashioned form of dry storage is the use of a root cellar. Depending on what you know about root cellars, you may have just had a flashback to some images in an old textbook of early American pioneers. Maybe you pictured a dark, dingy, perhaps even haunted, dungeon-like room filled with onions, garlic, and potatoes. The truth is that, because of the way our modern homes are built, most of them cannot sustain the demands of a proper root cellar.

On average, root cellars were traditionally kept between 32°F and 40°F along with a higher humidity of 80% to 90%. Another requirement of a proper root cellar is to have good ventilation; keeping the air moving prevents opportunistic bacteria and fungi from growing on the produce. The ideal root cellar is also fairly dark most of the time, especially when no one is inside. This is because light itself can trigger an enzyme reaction, resulting in the deterioration of your food. In summary, low temperatures and good ventilation keep unwanted organisms from growing, while high humidity locks in the moisture of the produce. All these characteristics are what make root cellars an ideal place to store fresh produce!

Now, under the ideal scenario, fruits and vegetables in a root cellar could last up to 6 months. But most people don't have official root cellars and it's even harder to have one of these cellars in the south because of the climate. Don't lose hope though! There are other ways that you can try to mimic the conditions, given the above requirements. Often people use a corner of their basement or a closet in their house as their version of a root cellar. Some helpful equipment includes storage boxes, crates, or styrofoam containers to contain the vegetables. Both a thermometer to monitor the room temperature and a humidity gauge to keep track of the moisture are also helpful. If you don't have space in your house and you live in a fairly cool climate, you can use a large bin such as a trash can or a large receptacle and dig a hole in the ground before placing the bin in the ground and filling it with your produce.

So, what can you store in a root cellar? Well, as the name implies, root vegetables do extremely well. This would include your carrots, potatoes, and radishes. Onions and cabbage also do very well. You can also store fruits like apples and oranges. The key to maintaining a root cellar is staying vigilant and checking on your produce fairly often to ensure that there isn't microorganism growth and that the plants are maintaining their freshness. The earlier you catch a problem with your produce, the better you will be able to troubleshoot the likely culprit. If your vegetables are shriveling, there likely isn't enough humidity. If they are becoming too soft, the temperature may be too high to lock in the crispness. If you notice mold, check your ventilation. And if you notice your food is spoiling faster than anticipated, try adjusting any potential light sources.

## *Canning*

Arguably the most popular type of long-term food preservation is canning. Now, if you're completely new to this process, when you think of canning, you likely think of the rows and rows of metal cans sitting on the shelves in your local grocery store. However, canning actually has nothing to do with the type of container that the food is preserved in; many gardeners can produce in glass jars, because they can be reused more easily than metal containers.

**Water bath canning** is the most beginner friendly. Coincidentally, it is also the most forgiving. You don't need very much fancy equipment outside of what you already have in your kitchen. Canning is best for foods that are acidic or have a pH that is less than or equal to 4.5. Typically, this type of canning will be good for your fruits, jellies, and tomatoes. For most canning, you can just use a regular pot on your stove. All you have to do is make sure the bottoms of the jars are not directly touching the bottom of the pot. There should be space for at least 1 to 2" of water above the jars.

**Pressure canning is another method**. This method is best for foods that have a pH that is greater than or equal to 4.6. While many foods fall in this category, some foods should never be pressure canned, including broccoli and summer squash.

One of the biggest fears people have when learning how to can is concerns about botulism. If you are unfamiliar, it is a potentially fatal illness caused by a type of nerve toxin produced by a bacteria called Clostridium botulinum that can live in soil and on produce. When food is not canned correctly, this bacteria may not be killed in the process. It is incredibly rare with today's modern tools that can aid with the process, however. Following proper guidelines for canning will drastically reduce the chances of this ever being a problem. At the end of the day: when in doubt, throw it out! Your health is not worth risking for a can of homegrown green beans, no matter how good the harvest was.

## *Freezing*

Perhaps the easiest and most overlooked method is simply freezing. In general, fruits and vegetables will last about 8 to 12 months in the freezer. Once there, it would be best for you to clearly label the packages and perhaps put them in order by the date on which they were frozen. For the best quality, you should freeze the food at 0°F as soon as you are done packaging. If the produce is warm from the climate in your greenhouse, wait until it cools to room temperature before putting it in the freezer.

This method of food preservation could be considered a luxury thanks to the convenience of modern appliances. With just a few quick steps, you can go from the garden to the freezer and then right to the table. Even though there is less prep work than other methods of preservation, there are a few big things to keep in mind. First, it's important to have an idea of what generally will not freeze well. Some examples of produce with a poor freezer quality include cabbage, lettuce, celery, radish, endive, fresh tomatoes, and potatoes. If in doubt, you can test a small sample before doing a whole batch and see how you like the consistency.

Some fruits and vegetables require blanching. Blanching is the process by which you partially cook produce before quickly submerging it into an ice bath, which not only stops the cooking process but preserves many of the nutrients that would otherwise break down if it were to continue cooking. This is helpful for produce like asparagus and broccoli.

**Make sure that your containers are air-tight and leak-proof.** The container should be able to withstand low temperatures without cracking. Rigid containers like glass and plastic are often used because of their ease of organization and stacking. However, if using glass, be aware that it is more prone to cracking in low temperatures. To decrease that chance, leave a bit of extra space at the top to allow for expansion. If using plastic freezer bags, try to remove as much air from the bag before freezing. Reducing the amount of air and ensuring a tight seal will lock in the freshness and decrease the chances of freezer burn.

## *Drying*

**Dehydration** is an excellent way to preserve food because it's a fairly simple process, and it allows you to have a shelf-stable food product for about a year. Dehydration is the process of removing water from food, which reduces the ability of bacteria and fungi to grow, thus making it shelf stable. Using this process, you can remove about 80% to 90% of the moisture in your food. Just as with other methods of food preservation, there are multiple ways that you can achieve food dehydration.

Perhaps the oldest method is good ol' **sun-drying**: leaving your produce outside in the sun to allow nature to take its course. This method works best in areas with low humidity and high heat. However, there are a few other ways to help the drying process. If you live in an area that is unnaturally dry, for example, there are screens that you can purchase that allow for proper airflow during sun-drying.

Another option - closely related to sun drying - is **air drying**. The main difference between air drying and sun drying is that air drying is done mostly in the shade. This method is useful for more delicate products like greens and herbs. A different version of this involves using your oven. This could be an option for gardeners who want to experiment but may not be ready to purchase a fancy dehydrator.

The main drawback to an oven is that you need to make sure that your oven will get to a low enough temperature to dehydrate the food rather than cook the food. This means it must get to around less than 140°F. Some of the herbs you may be growing require an even lower temperature closer to 95°F. The other drawback to using an oven is that it's not a year-round device! Keeping the oven on in the house for long periods of time during the summer can make the home unbearable.

Perhaps the most convenient method is using an electric dehydrator. These are usually fairly affordable and efficient and are equipped with a fan and heat generator which aids in the drying process.

Now that we've explored a few different methods, we should talk about how you prepare your food for dehydration. This depends on what exactly you're dehydrating. For example, some foods may require the skin to be peeled off prior to dehydration. Others may need to be sliced thinly or minced into very fine pieces. For fruits that are prone to browning, like apples, you may want to dip the fruit in lemon juice before proceeding with dehydration. Though not absolutely necessary for taste, this will help preserve the color, giving it a more aesthetically pleasing finish.

After you've finished dehydrating and collecting everything, the next step is to store the dehydrated foods in air-tight jars or vacuum-sealed pouches.

## *Fermenting*

One last option for long-term preservation is **fermenting or pickling food**. As usual, many of these components are adjusted based on what you are pickling or fermenting. For example, fruit is usually heated in a simple syrup with lemon juice or vinegar added, but the process of dill pickling is much different.

It's important that you find a clear recipe if you choose to pickle or ferment any of your produce. This has to do just as much with safety as it does with the taste and quality of the product. Acid is important to prevent the formation of bacteria.

To start, make sure that you pick only the best produce that shows no signs of rot or damage. Use either pickling salt or canning salt. To add sweetness, you can use white or brown sugar. As far as vinegar, white vinegar is usually the preferred option since the color is more attractive. Vinegar with 5% acidity is suggested.

You may have to do some research on what chemicals can best help with keeping the produce firm while pickled. Many people use food-grade lime and soak the vegetables in them before pickling.

To prevent the growth of microorganisms or spoilage, it's recommended that you **process your vegetable or fruit in a container of boiling water.** This helps to destroy any microorganisms or denature any enzymes that may be present before pickling. After this process, the produce should be stored in an airtight container. Usually, basic canning jars with self-sealing lids are used.

When fermenting, make sure that the produce is one to two inches beneath the brine while it is fermenting. The container should be set apart in a clean and dark location with a base room temperature of 60°F to 68°F for about two to three weeks. Foods that are fermented and properly prepared can usually last for about four to 18 months depending on the food and the quality of the preparation.

## Monitoring Your Harvest

Just because you have completed your harvest and storage doesn't mean that your work is through! Even after you've been able to can, freeze, or ferment your produce to last for a while, you'll want to keep a close eye on it. This is especially true if you plan on using it to make a profit.

A bit of organization will help with monitoring. It is helpful to label jars and packages with, at the minimum, the name of the item and the date it was prepared for storage (this is more important than the harvest date). You can organize the items in the order they were preserved for quick access. Periodic monitoring of your produce once or twice a week can help you catch any problems that may arise before they get out of hand. Picking up a jar and briefly shining a light through it can help you notice if there are any strange substances or cloudiness that was not present before. Go through your dry storage and make sure that there is no moisture on any bins or in the surrounding area. You can even take pictures when you check so that you can have something to compare it to for the next time. Doing these checks regularly can help you notice when anything is off so you can prevent your dry storage crops from collecting moisture and potentially sprouting or rotting.

It may be helpful to keep a simple log to document when and what you found while doing your weekly or biweekly check on your harvest. This way, you can tell if there is something new in a container or a jar that you did not notice before and if it is progressively getting worse. Any rotting or damaged produce that you find during this inspection should immediately be removed. Then, check the remaining produce for signs of similar issues.

Once you've gotten all of your fruits and vegetables into storage and have a good idea of what you'll have available for distribution, it's time to implement your business plan and see how you can pull a profit. This next chapter will address the business side of greenhouse gardening and opportunities you have to make a little extra cash on the side (or, begin the full-time job of a lifetime).

# Chapter 9:

# Pulling a Profit

This is where you get to see the results of your hard work. You've now harvested and stored your greenhouse produce! Congratulations! Perhaps you grew it only for yourself, or perhaps you grew it to sell, or maybe you just have a surplus from your harvest. Whatever the case, now is the time for us to talk about how you can use your greenhouse to pull a profit. There are a lot of different ways and methods to use your produce financially. This chapter will cover a few of those methods and explore how to make your greenhouse into a side business.

## Networking and Connection

Much of business is about who you know, and the backyard greenhouse business is no different. To find people to sell your produce to, you're going to have to get to know and connect with people. This means building relationships and being able to explain your product. This may require you to step outside of your comfort zone and explore creative avenues for meeting new people and understanding your audience.

### *Meeting Potential Customers*

Customers come in all forms. This means that you'll have to be creative with how you meet them. You can find potential customers anywhere. One of the easiest ways is to reach out to chefs and food industry professionals. Restaurant owners and chefs are always looking for farm-to-table produce. If your product is good, they may be interested in sourcing from you. You can also go to any local food community events and connect with people there. In some cases, you may find that you can open up a booth and advertise your product.

Speaking of booths, farmers markets and other such events are also great places to get to know people. You have everyday human beings who are coming to inspect your wares, but you also have business owners and other small restaurant workers who may be looking for quality products to use in their establishment.

You can also volunteer at different local food community events. Being part of the planning or implementation teams means you can meet like-minded people and get wind of the financial food climate of your area. A lot of these people are food advocates who are looking to change the way that we eat. If they hear that you grow your own vegetables and fruits with no pesticides or potentially harmful additives, I can guarantee you that they would be interested in having a conversation. Once you start getting to know people, keep shaking hands and attending events. The more people you know, the better!

## *Get To Know The Demand*

Knowing people is only half the battle, though: you also need to get to know the demand of your area. To do this, you may need to engage in some legwork. Find out where the restaurants in your area are getting their food. Are they locally sourced? Are they commercially sourced? In some cases, they may be shopping at local markets and buying bulk based on what's in season. Because you have a greenhouse, you can grow plants at any time during the year. Getting to know what local chefs or restaurant owners are looking for at key times can help you know how to plan your crop schedule and make sure that your produce is ready when their need is highest. For restaurant owners who aren't sourcing their food locally or are buying commercially, knowing that someone is available to work with them and provide them with regular produce that is pesticide-free and fresh can sway them to do business with you.

Find out what people like to eat that they have a hard time obtaining. In some regions, it may be harder to find winter vegetables. These can be more expensive or unavailable entirely. When you find vegetables that are in demand and not as readily available, you can attract restaurant owners and enthusiasts who want what you have.

## *Be Transparent*

People want to work with people that they know they can trust, and this includes business owners. The key here is to build trust through consistency over time. It is something that is earned.

One of the best ways to build trust is to come up with a plan and sit down with your potential customers to walk them through that plan. Show them pictures of your greenhouse and share with them how you maintain it and how you plant your crops. Be ready to articulate to them the soil composition as well as share a sample or two of the produce itself. Let them know what you can and cannot do as well as a realistic amount that you can produce for them per year. This sounds like a lot of work because it is. But coming prepared to a meeting like this will help to emphasize to your customer that you are serious and that you are transparent.

Likewise, as you are outlining all the things that you can do, make sure to let them know how you approach any potential risks. Come up with a plan for how to deal with a season where you lose plants due to blight or a pest outbreak. Let them know if there are any risks and clearly articulate what your expectations for them as a customer are. Do not commit to growing and producing seven orange trees if you know that you do not have the space or the time to be able to grow and develop those. Make sure to be fair in your pricing and to let them know upfront how much they can pay for a certain amount of produce.

## Designing Your Business

How you design your business will dictate how well it is executed. A well-planned business can provide you with customers and income for years, and it can also provide peace of mind and less effort in the long run. There are many different ways that you can run a business and we will cover a few of them in this section. Keep in mind, that this list is not exhaustive nor is it a single choice. Many backyard gardeners choose multiple options. Educate yourself on the different opportunities available and make them work for you.

### *Modified CSA*

CSA is a **community supported agriculture** group. This is where individuals in a community choose to support a local gardener. These are usually done on larger scales, but you can also do one on a much smaller scale. In typical CSAs, people purchase a provision of the harvest well-before the growing season starts. In exchange, the investor gets a regular supply of everything that the grower produces. This helps to offset any of the risks that the grower faces like drought, pestilence, or disease.

On a smaller scale, this may mean that you are connecting with your neighbors, nearby apartment complexes, and other local communities. In exchange for their buy-in, you deliver your produce to them at specific times and places. Or, you can have them pick up the produce at a specific time throughout the week. When you begin, people might be more skeptical and not as willing to buy in (don't worry, that will change over time). In this case, you can provide them with this service on an as-needed basis. This arrangement becomes especially effective when you can survey the populace you serve and get an idea of what they would like to see as far as a product.

## *Online Market*

If you are more tech-savvy and want to start exploring some of the digital options available, the online market is a growing and expanding option. There are many people connected to the Internet and, especially with the COVID-19 pandemic, businesses are moving online. People are spending more time on the web and purchasing more products digitally than ever; it is almost impossible for someone to have a business without having some sort of online presence. Since people are online already, why not give them a place to buy fresh produce while surfing the web? Using the Internet, you can sell products to potential customers directly.

Again, an online presence is almost required for any business to truly be successful. To that end, it is especially useful to have a webpage that, at the very least, tells people that you are growing and selling produce. If you wanted to, you could make it so that your surveys, sign-ups, and payments for a CSA run through your webpage. At the very least, you should have a page that outlines your products and has pictures of your greenhouse and your amazing setup.

You can also sell your product exclusively on the Internet, or perhaps you want to have a hybrid where you have products sold in person, but also the opportunity for people to request products delivered or for pick up online. Maybe you want to send bulk products to restaurants and other organizations. You can often package any produce that require refrigeration in containers that will preserve the cold temperature. You can also package these with dry ice to keep your produce fresh and crisp.

For some people, Internet marketing is more attractive than in-person marketing, as you don't have the same real estate or effort that you would have to manage in a physical establishment. Although there is still time and energy that you must put in, it is not nearly as substantial as a brick-and-mortar building or farmer's market stall.

## *Farmer's Markets*

There is something very relaxing about going to a farmer's market and looking at all the fresh produce. In fact, many families and community members use farmer's markets as a way to get out, feel connected, and practice healthy living. As these events continue to grow in popularity, you may find that they provide a great opportunity to make a few extra dollars. Make sure you do your research beforehand, however, as most farmer's markets come with regulations and require preparation.

The first thing to decide is what produce you're going to sell at the farmer's market. If you take some of the advice above and connect with your community, you can find out what some of the popular items are and prepare to sell those at the next farmer's market. You can also bring whatever your surplus harvest is, especially if you don't feel like going through the long-term preservation process. Make sure you're aware of any rules that your farmer's market might have for produce and how it's sold, packaged, or maintained.

Make sure to do all your budgeting and business planning beforehand. Determine how much you need to charge to profit, and make sure to set your budget for renting a stall, buying tables or seats, storage, and promotional items like signs and flyers, as well as any food permits that you might need to have. Doing your research for your particular farmers market can help you determine what costs you will need to incur to be ready.

Finally, make sure that you come up with a good name for your booth and register it with any farmer's market officials. This is also a good time to ask about permits or licenses that you will need to sell your products. The sooner you get this process done, the sooner you can begin to plan where you want to be and how you want to position yourself in the farmer's market.

Before you get to the market, take some time to practice breaking down and setting up your booth. There's nothing worse than losing customers because you had to take a few extra hours to get ready on the day of the market. Practice at home and use that opportunity to figure out how to make your booth more attractive and approachable. Do you want something that will invite people to sit down and ask questions? Consider what kind of produce you want closest to the front of the booth to show off the best of your harvest.

At the end of the day, remember that, although this is a business, it's also about relationships. Show kindness to the people who approach your booth and engage with them. Get to know them and use that opportunity to determine what they are most interested in. This can give you ideas about what kinds of plants to begin producing for the next farmer's market. Just as you practiced when you partnered with another business, be transparent and let them know that these plants were produced in a greenhouse as well as how you composed the soil, designed your space, and how you maintained them. Part of the attraction of farmers markets is getting produce that you know as part of a healthy lifestyle.

## *Personal*

The last option is to start your own business independent of any of the previous tools. This may mean selling from your driveway or on the side of the road. This can also mean buying or leasing a building and creating a storefront for your products. This could even be going door-to-door and providing catalogs to neighbors and businesses of your wares. This requires a very intentional mindset and skillset and is not for everyone. However, if you want absolute control over everything in your business model, this is a good way to get that.

Also, keep in mind that starting one way doesn't mean that you can't change and adjust. Perhaps you start with an online market and then, after some success, you decide to invest in a storefront. Or maybe you start with offering your wares at local farmer's markets, and then, once your community is more aware of your business, you begin offering personal deliveries. All of these are great options to expand your greenhouse business and grow it into something unique.

If you choose to start your own business, make future plans for how you'd like to expand, unless you plan to keep it basic. Once you begin to get some traction and you have more regular orders, your customers will begin to depend on you to provide produce. This can get overwhelming, and you may need to bring in some help. If you have family, this is a great way to get them involved and active. However, if it's just you, think about hiring some local assistance if needed. You may need someone to help you with the online purchasing process; perhaps you know someone tech-savvy who can check in to make sure that orders are being fulfilled; or maybe you know a really social somebody who would be in their element selling at a storefront. In any case, thinking about where you can expand your business is a good first step to making a greater profit and getting a farther reach.

For a lot of people, though, this is simply not their thing. They started a garden because they wanted a place to relax and enjoy themselves, and if you're not interested in expanding your business (or starting one at all!) that's completely fine. Most likely, you started your greenhouse journey for yourself, and that's how it should always stay.

If you do decide to grow a business, here is a free, printable sample budget form where you can chart your income and expenses as you go.

# MONTHLY GREENHOUSE BUDGET

| BUDGET GOAL: | MONTH/YEAR: |
|---|---|

## GREENHOUSE INCOME

| Date | Description | Amount |
|---|---|---|
|  |  |  |
|  |  |  |
|  |  |  |
|  |  |  |
|  |  |  |

**TOTAL:**

## GREENHOUSE EXPENSES

| Type (Veg, Fruit, Herb, Supplies) | Description | Quantity | Cost |
|---|---|---|---|

|   |   |   |   |
|---|---|---|---|
|   |   |   |   |
|   |   |   |   |
|   |   |   |   |
|   |   |   |   |
|   |   |   |   |
| **TOTAL:** |   |   |   |

## FINAL BALANCE

|  | Estimated | Actual | Difference |
|---|---|---|---|
| Income |  |  |  |
| Expenses |  |  |  |
| Total Left |  |  |  |

## Chapter 10:

# Making it Last

Now you've got the greenhouse of your dreams: a place where you can relax, get fresh food, engage in a breathtaking hobby, and maybe even turn a profit. The last step is to maintain that momentum and continue growing. When it comes to greenhouse gardening, sustainability can be a challenge.

This section will explore seasonal growing as well as how to select your plants for extended and consistent growth. Full disclosure: most of this information will be generalized, as everyone structures their greenhouse differently and all of us have a different combination of plants, soil, lights, and other accessories. As you go through this final section, consider how you can integrate some of these ideas to help your greenhouse continue to produce and profit year-round.

## Fail to Plan, Plan to Fail

We've come full circle! We started this journey with a period of preparation, and now, to continue the journey, we need to enter another period of preparation. Planning your year-round garden is critical for success, especially if you intend to produce particular crops at particular times.

To better plan your year-round greenhouse, take time to get to know your garden. Do regular walkthroughs, taking notice of the sun cycle, movement of pests through the garden, and how your crops respond to different changes in temperature and humidity. Understand and connect to the various processes taking place in that space day after day.

Your garden is not the only thing you'll need to put effort into for sustainability. Your greenhouse doesn't thrive without YOU! Sometimes the work can get hard and discouraging. Spending quality time in your greenhouse for its own sake will not only help you get to know your garden better but remind you why you started gardening in the first place.

# Year-Round Production

Planting crops year-round is how you get a consistent flow of produce on a regular basis. This is also how you continue to keep the soil fresh and nourished. If you're starting a business, you must know how to keep your crops producing throughout the year by carefully using your greenhouse and planning your schedule.

## *Alternating Crops*

Alternating crops (also known as crop rotation) is a technique commonly used in commercial farming. This can protect and enhance crop productivity.

Crop rotation is the practice of growing different crops in the same place over several different seasons. This helps return nutrients into the ground without hormones or other supplements. This process also helps to disrupt any disease cycles that may be trying to establish themselves in the soil while getting rid of any habitat conditions for pests and parasites.

There are some risks with this process, however. If you don't do it correctly, you can accidentally cross-contaminate your produce. You'll need to be intentional about which crops you're planting, as well as when and how. Anything that you have planted prior will influence what's coming next.

When you rotate and plant crops with different root systems, you enhance the soil. Rotating plants that have short root systems with crops that have long root systems gives the different layers of the soil a chance to regain nutrients. The different root structures also help to increase the biomass as well as the natural diversity of nutrients in the soil. Certain crops help increase the organic matter and nitrogen content of soil composition. They interact in a symbiotic relationship with bacteria, which produce different nutrients when they come into contact with those root systems.

In order to know which crops and bacteria are symbiotic, you'll need to do research to find the relationship between your current produce and the ecosystem beneath the ground.

Ideally, you should rotate every three or four years. An example of crop rotation is taking nightshade crops like tomatoes and eggplants and rotating them with gourds like cucumbers and squash. These family groups are also prone to different sets of diseases and are less likely to cross-contaminate. Crop rotation like this is essential to help create a balanced garden system.

## *Stagger Planting*

Staggered planting is a technique that involves sowing seeds a little bit at a time over an extended period. This extends the season, allowing your plants to grow in a staggered fashion, and helps to keep you from getting overwhelmed with a large amount of produce all at once. If that happens, some of that produce may be wasted, or you may be stuck with a lot of stored food.

Whatever the case, staggered planting also allows you to keep providing fresh vegetables for all your consumers. If people are expecting crops at a certain time, you'd ideally be able to give them the newest and freshest crops possible. Staggered planting also allows you to pick and choose which crops will be available to them based on their interest.

By stagger planting, you'll have plants of the same type at different stages of maturity at different times. Staggered planting is only limited by growing seasons, which we can regulate as greenhouse owners. Using this method, you will always have a new batch just behind the last.

Staggered planting is also another way of defending against disease and pests. Let's say that you have your first batch of tomatoes, however, that batch of tomatoes has been wiped out in a blight. Fortunately, you don't have to worry as much, because you have a new set of young plants already starting to produce fruit. Although you won't get back your first round of plants, this new set can hopefully step up and fill the gap.

Staggered planting will take some advanced planning. You'll have to allocate extra space in your garden for staggered crops, after which you'll plan however much crop you need per week and plant that much several times over the course of a season. After you've planted your first crop, you wait however many days (10, 14, 21, etc.) and then plant the next crop. This allows you adequate time to grow and care for the first crop, as well as prepare the second crop.

To pull this off, you'll need to have all your planting needs met before you begin. This means any soil that needs to be amended or supplemented should be ready to go, and this also means that you should stockpile seeds during the spring months for use throughout the year. Any seed soaking time should also be included in your timetable.

## *Planting in Season*

Of course, this section should be obvious. One way to consistently have crops throughout the years is to plant them within the season that they grow best. That means planning ahead and being ready to plant your summer crops during the summer, as well as your hardy or cold weather crops during the fall and winter seasons. If your area tends to have bitter winters and you don't want to hike up your heating bill by providing heat to your greenhouse during this period, you can give your garden a rest and simply prepare crops over the next few months for planting.

Sometimes people become discouraged when they are unable to grow a particular crop because it only grows in a specific season, as they want to grow something that they (or a customer) are craving. But seasonal planting makes sense, especially as an example of sustainable planting so you can have access to fresh foods year-round.

In fact, the ideal is to be able to eat as many fresh fruits and vegetables as possible and use various preservation or sales methods for the surplus. There are also several benefits to seasonal eating, including an appreciation for the fruits or vegetables that grow during that time. For example, if cherries are your favorite fruit, then you probably look forward to them coming to stores every summer. Summer cherries absolutely taste better than winter cherries! Seasonal planting means that you can enjoy the best produce during their peak seasons for the most optimal nutrition.

Like all the others, this takes planning to make sure that you have crops on hand for every season and that they are being planted and seeded in advance, especially if you're planning to transplant them.

You can also plan for seasons by selecting perennial plants that you know will produce over the course of a lifetime. Popular examples include strawberries, blueberries, and blackberries. Again, you will need to plan for these plants, knowing that they will eventually produce fruit come their target season. That means you'll have to keep watch over them and the soil that they grow in throughout the off-season. In addition, perennial vegetables such as asparagus and rhubarb often take more time to establish and may require more patience. Their harvests also tend to be smaller than the harvest of annual crops during the first harvest season.

At the end of each season, take time to think about what you've grown that you want more of. Once you've done that, you can think more about staggered planting. Don't forget to pay close attention to the climate since that will impact what you can plant.

# Conclusion

By this point, you're probably bubbling over with ideas on how to create your ideal greenhouse. We've covered everything from greenhouse designs to different business models you can use to sell your produce. Along the way, I hope you realize that, while there are definitely some physical and financial benefits to owning a greenhouse, there are also plenty of mental and wellness benefits too.

As you continue to explore the creation of your greenhouse experience, I encourage you to start small and grow from there. Often, we want to take all these wonderful ideas and immediately run off and begin a monumental greenhouse endeavor. We want to produce our own fruits and vegetables, sell the excess, and come up with schedules that allow us to meet these goals. While all that is noble, it is often unrealistic.

The truth is, if you are just starting your gardening experience (or your greenhouse gardening experience) it's important that you start small to understand all the concepts and get the hang of the process before expanding. That's why, in earlier chapters, I encouraged you to find a greenhouse that is slightly larger than what you assume you will need. In fact, find a greenhouse that takes up all the space that you have allotted for it. This allows you the opportunity to expand as you get the greenhouse bug and want to do more.

A greenhouse can be a very inviting place. Surrounded by fruits and vegetables, as well as the aromas and fresh scents that come with them, you really can create your own world. As you seek to be an effective greenhouse gardener, take time to enjoy the journey. Create a space that is all your own! Bring in some chairs and a table, have a place where you can sit with a book or journal. If you have a smaller greenhouse, set up furniture nearby that still allows you to take in the greenhouse experience while remaining comfortable. Experiment with different times of day and figure out when you are most comfortable in that environment. Do you enjoy sitting out underneath the stars at night? Or do you love the early mornings when the weather is still cool and the sunlight is streaming through the tempered glass?

A greenhouse does not have to be all work. In fact, if you find yourself forcing yourself to be present and complete your tasks, then you may need to cut back on what you're doing and reevaluate. Gardening should be fun and interesting. As you learn more about your plants, you learn more about yourself. You learn about persistence and patience. You learn to celebrate the small moments when you see your first seedling sprout, as well as the big moments when you pull that first potato out of the ground. Most of all, you learn that you are capable and that, with just a little bit of effort, you can create something beautiful out of something small.

Consider inviting family and friends to have this experience with you, too. For many of them, this will be a new and exciting opportunity to be part of growing something from nothing. That same benefits you've experienced should be shared with other people. You'll find that, as you do, you're also rewarded with the positive feeling of being part of a community working together.

Invite your family to sit with you in your greenhouse. Something as simple as spending time in your oasis of agriculture can spark unique conversations and an interest in gardening. You can also share fruits and vegetables with others as you grow them. Many times, you will have a surplus, and homegrown produce makes a great and easy gift. The best part is that you don't even have to wait for a holiday! It's a great way to get to know your neighbors and a fun way to do something nice for your friends and family.

A greenhouse is a wonderful tool that allows you to experience the joys of gardening year-round. By managing a greenhouse, you provide yourself with a healthy source of fresh produce, while also strengthening your mental health and mindfulness. I want to encourage you to continue your journey of greenhouse gardening. Continue to learn, grow, experiment, and enjoy all the wonders that greenhouse gardening offers.

If you enjoyed these Greenhouse Gardening Tips then you are a perfect fit to join our likeminded and passionate

**Abundance Greenhouse & Gardening Community**

on Facebook!

https://www.facebook.com/groups/1637128983319044

and

Kindly leave a review on Amazon!

# References

Bradbury, K. (2010, November 5). Storing and Preserving Your Garden Harvest. *GrowVeg*. https://www.growveg.com/guides/storing-and-preserving-your-garden-harvest/

Conti, M. (2022, January 7). 10 Backyard Greenhouses You Can Buy Online. *HGTV*. https://www.hgtv.com/outdoors/gardens/planting-and-maintenance/greenhouses-you-can-buy-online

Dawe, J. (2018, October 10). Greenhouse Cleaning and Maintenance for Beginners. *Eartheasy Guides & Articles*. https://learn.eartheasy.com/articles/greenhouse-cleaning-and-maintenance-for-beginners/

Deanna. (2019, October 18). *A* Beginner's Guide to Using a Hobby Greenhouse. *Homestead and Chill*. https://homesteadandchill.com/beginners-guide-using-hobby-greenhouse/

G, B. (2021, April 23). How to Build a Greenhouse. *Lowes*. https://www.lowes.com/n/how-to/how-to-build-a-greenhouse

Garden & Greenhouse. (2022a, January 14). How Does a Greenhouse Work? *Garden & Greenhouse*. https://www.gardenandgreenhouse.net/how-does-a-greenhouse-work/

Garden & Greenhouse. (2022b, February 3). Tips for Choosing the Perfect Spot for Your Greenhouse. *Garden & Greenhouse*. https://www.gardenandgreenhouse.net/tips-for-choosing-the-perfect-spot-for-your-greenhouse/

Grant, G. (2022, January 5). Sooty Mold. *TylerPaper.com*. https://tylerpaper.com/lifestyle/sooty-mold/article_dbc2089a-4cde-11ec-ac95-f3c93e2c1437.html

Greenhouse Emporium. (2017, February 24). Greenhouse Gardening For Beginners - Where do I start? *Greenhouse Emporium*. https://greenhouseemporium.com/blogs/greenhouse-gardening/greenhouse-gardening-for-beginners/

Greenhouse Garden Center. (n.d.). Fruits, Vegetables & Herbs. *Greenhouse Garden Center*. https://greenhousegardencenter.com/garden-guides/fruits-vegetables-herbs/

Helmer, J. (2020, November 4). *ICYMI: How To Start a CSA*. Growing Produce. https://www.growingproduce.com/farm-marketing/how-to-start-a-csa/

Holden, E. (2019, March 20). Pesticide residues found in 70% of produce sold in US even after washing. *The Guardian*. https://www.theguardian.com/environment/2019/mar/20/pesticide-residues-produce-even-after-washing-us

Leech, J. (2017, June 3). 10 Delicious Herbs and Spices With Powerful Health Benefits. *Healthline*. https://www.healthline.com/nutrition/10-healthy-herbs-and-spices

Lowin, R. (2020, February 24). These Budget-Friendly DIY Greenhouses Will Beautify Your Backyard. *Country Living*. https://www.countryliving.com/gardening/g2506/diy-greenhouses/

Michaels, E. (2012, August 15). *5 Top Tips for Greenhouse Maintenance by Ewan Michaels*. Hartley Botanic. https://hartley-botanic.co.uk/magazine/5-top-tips-for-greenhouse-maintenance-by-ewan-michaels/

Riley, D., Sparks, A., Srinivasan, R., Kennedy, G., Fonsah, G., Scott, J., & Olson, S. (2018). Chapter 3 - Thrips: Biology, Ecology, and Management. W. Wakil, G. E. Brust, & T.M. Perring (Eds.), *Sustainable Management of Arthropod Pests of Tomato.* (1st ed., pp. 49-71). Academic Press. https://www.sciencedirect.com/science/article/pii/B9780128024416000036

Rush, M. (n.d.). How to Start in the Farmer's Market Business. *Small Business - Chron.com.* https://smallbusiness.chron.com/start-farmers-market-business-3445.html

The Home Depot. (n.d.). How to Build a Greenhouse. *The Home Depot.* https://www.homedepot.com/c/ah/how-to-build-a-greenhouse/9ba683603be9fa5395fab905443ffce

Gaus, A. E., Zuroweste, R. (2017, May). Vegetable Harvest and Storage. *Extension.missouri.edu.* https://extension.missouri.edu/publications/g6226

Truini, J. (2019, January 28). How to Build a Greenhouse. *Popular Mechanics.* https://www.popularmechanics.com/home/a26063857/diy-greenhouse/

Waterworth, K. (2021, February 1). Greenhouse Gardening Supplies: What Are Common Supplies For A Greenhouse. *Gardening Know How.* https://www.gardeningknowhow.com/special/greenhouses/greenhouse-gardening-supplies.htm

Williams, P. (2017, July 27). Two types of temperature & humidity control. Greenhouse Management. https://www.greenhousemag.com/article/two-types-of-temperature--humidity-control/

# Image References

Avamotive, J. (2018). Interior view of glass house [Photograph]. pexels.com. https://www.pexels.com/photo/interior-view-of-glass-house-1034902/

Baldwin, I. (2015). Ripe peaches on a tree [Photograph]. unsplash.com. https://unsplash.com/photos/f7FwHomDgzg

Boozer, D. (2018). Strawberries growing in garden [Photograph]. unsplash.com. https://unsplash.com/photos/-jQZ6AHtuWM

Braxmeier, H. (2013). Thyme real culinary herbs [Photograph]. pixabay.com. https://pixabay.com/photos/thyme-real-thyme-culinary-herbs-115349/

Bresson, R. (2016). Corn cob in field [Photograph]. pixabay.com. https://pixabay.com/photos/corn-food-field-vegetable-corncob-1690387/

Claire, R. (2019). Flowers in greenhouse in sunlight [Photograph]. pexel.com. https://www.pexels.com/photo/flowers-in-green-house-in-sunlight-4577365/

Foret, V. (2018). Portrait of rosemary [Photograph]. unsplash.com. https://unsplash.com/photos/R8Ct7Macnus

G, G. (2017). Kale in field [Photograph]. pixabay.com. https://pixabay.com/photos/meal-food-vegetables-kale-cabbage-2865208/

Garget, J. (2020). Seedlings growing in garden [Photograph]. pixabay.com. https://pixabay.com/photos/seedling-gardening-greenhouse-5009286/

Hanson, C. (2015). Lacto-fermentation pickling [Photograph]. pixabay.com. https://pixabay.com/photos/lacto-fermentation-pickling-861551/

Helena. (2016). Freestanding greenhouse [Photograph]. pixabay.com. https://pixabay.com/photos/greenhouse-summer-grow-green-1192872/

Jackson, D. (2016). Farm wood vintage farm [Photograph]. pexels.com. https://www.pexels.com/photo/food-wood-vintage-farm-6611594/

Joaquin. (2016). Cold frame greenhouse [Photograph]. pixabay.com. https://pixabay.com/photos/mini-greenhouse-lettuce-vegetable-1890254/

Kemper, J. (2020). Harvested carrots [Photograph]. unsplash.com. https://unsplash.com/photos/iPiXhoMUcV8

Śliwka, D. (2020). Bacterial soft rot cauliflower [Photography]. pixabay.com. https://pixabay.com/photos/bacterial-soft-rot-cauliflower-5505301/

Spiske, M. (2018). Cucumber growing in garden [Photograph]. unsplash.com. https://unsplash.com/photos/fPLSD4mz7II

Spiske, M. (2019). Homegrown basil herb [Photograph]. unsplash.com. https://unsplash.com/photos/S6ieGQAD5pU

Spratt, A. (2018). Garden tools in a greenhouse/glass house [Photograph]. unsplash.com. https://unsplash.com/photos/q_WvgGKONQI

Wende, W. (2020). Powdery mildew on leaf [Photograph]. pixabay.com. https://pixabay.com/photos/mildew-nettle-mushroom-spores-5251894/

Winkler, M. (2016). Local farmer's market [Photograph]. pixabay.com. https://pixabay.com/photos/market-vegetable-market-1558658/

Made in the USA
Columbia, SC
19 March 2025

442fbbc7-9883-42ea-8f26-47090fead269R01